BURGER GREEK BUR
BREAKFAST
USTARD SEED
BURGER OPEN-FACE
CHICKEN BURGER BL
TURKEY CLUB BURG
OSTRICH BACON BUR
SEARED TUNA BURG
BLE SALMON TARTAR
BURGER SALMON FILA
ET BURGER BRAZILIA
SHRIMP BURGER CRA
RS MAC AND CHEES
BURGER ROASTED S

BURGER BAR

BUR

BURGER BAR

Build Your Own Ultimate Burgers

Hubert Keller
with Penelope Wisner

 JOHN WILEY & SONS, INC.

To whomever hungers for the ultimate burger

Copyright © 2009 by Hubert Keller. All rights reserved
Photography © 2009 by Bill Milne.
Published by John Wiley & Sons, Inc., Hoboken, New Jersey
Published simultaneously in Canada

For general information on our other products and services or for technical support,
please contact our Customer Care Department within the United States at
(800) 762-2974, outside the United States at (317) 572-3993 or fax (317) 572-4002.
Wiley also publishes its books in a variety of electronic formats. Some content that
appears in print may not be available in electronic books. For more information about
Wiley products, visit our web site at www.wiley.com.

Library of Congress Cataloging-in-Publication Data
Keller, Hubert.
 Burger Bar: build your own ultimate burgers / Hubert Keller with Penelope Wisner.
    p. cm.
 Includes index.
 ISBN 978-0-470-18767-8 (cloth : alk. paper)
 1. Hamburgers. 2. Burger Bar (Restaurant) I. Wisner, Penelope. II. Title.
 TX749.5.B43K45 2009
 641.84'—dc22
                              2008012269

Design by Debbie Glasserman

Printed in China
10 9 8 7 6 5 4 3 2 1

CONTENTS

ACKNOWLEDGMENTS

To the entire team at Burger Bar, a big thank-you. I wish readers could stand in the kitchen and watch all your hard work, listen to the waiters and waitresses as they describe bun, bacon, and beef choices to guests, and watch through the window of the butcher shop to see every single burger get hand shaped. Readers would marvel at all that must come together to create a "simple" burger. And you might tell them, as you have before, "But this is not just a simple burger bar." It would take pages and pages to name all those who have contributed in countless and important ways to bring about this book. But there are some whom I would like to single out. To all the rest of you, I am no less grateful.

First and foremost, I want to express my gratitude to my wife and business partner, Chantal Keller. She has trusted and supported me as we have moved from continent to continent and undertaken new ventures. We have developed Burger Bar together from the very first telephone call that set us on the path of this new idea.

To Maurice Rouas, my friend and business partner of more than twenty years, with whom I could say—if it were not for Chantal—that we have a perfect marriage.

To Penni Wisner, my writing partner. Since we first met, Chantal and I have felt a wonderful bond with her. She has a gift for translating not just my ideas, but also the flavors and textures of my food, into colorful and evocative language. She has poured her tremendous energy and care into each word and teaspoon measurement.

To Bill Milne, photographer and friend, and his assistant, Chad MacDonald. Bill's humor, tact, and understanding made our work together flow naturally. I so appreciate the talent through which he transformed my dishes into the delicious images on these pages.

To Laurent Pillard, now the corporate chef of Burger Bar and Sleek Steakhouse/Ultra-Lounge. He was there before Burger Bar was a glint in anyone's eye, and has been instrumental throughout the development and expansion of Burger Bar. Laurent has given unstintingly of his creative energy with patience, understanding, and humor. And he has stood with me at the stove through the many long days and nights of cooking for photography. I cannot imagine a better man to have to "guard my back."

To Lisa Gourgeon, who does such a great job as the general manager of Burger Bar. Her professionalism and personal zeal keep Burger Bar moving from strength to strength.

To Stephen Mitchel, my friend and designer. When I told him we had three months to create Burger Bar's personality, he stepped up and created its graphic elements.

To Rick Richardson, the chef de cuisine of Fleur de Lys SF, who has worked with me since our days at Roger Vergé's San Francisco restaurant, Sutter 500. Way back then, we featured Rick's Burger on the menu.

I would also like to thank Fred Hill, my agent, and Linda Ingroia, my editor, for their belief and support. Also, at Wiley, I thank Ava Wilder, production editor, for her careful attention to detail; Jeff Faust, cover art director; Gypsy Lovett, publicity manager and Michael Friedberg, marketing manager. Designer Debbie Glasserman, created a beautiful, modern look for the book.

Thanks, too, to Joseph Arias, Clyde Burney, Marcus Joseph Garcia, Remberto Garcia, Yvette Landau, Tobias Peach, Bill Richardson, Gilberto Villarreal, and the Fleur de Lys teams in San Francisco and Las Vegas. I am so proud of and grateful to you all.

Before there was a Burger Bar, there was an empty space in the Mandalay Bay's shopping plaza, Mandalay Place. Many thank-yous go to Mandalay Bay for their continued support of Burger Bar and Fleur de Lys LV.

INTRO

The whole world recognizes The Burger's iconic status. But here in America, the relationship turns personal. The look and taste of the ideal burger—patty, bun, and sides—vary according to the diner. But all agree that burgers must satisfy the body and the soul. Friends and colleagues have often teased me: "What does a French chef know about burgers?" I had been the chef/owner, with partner Maurice Rouas and my wife, Chantal, of our four-star San Francisco Fleur de Lys restaurant for twenty years and had eaten perhaps three burgers in my life. Yet, quite suddenly and unexpectedly, in 2004 Laurent Pillard and I—two French chefs—found ourselves opening Burger Bar in Las Vegas, a hip, fun, casual, and thoroughly modern spot dedicated to creating the ultimate burger experience.

No one really knew what to expect. And certainly we did not imagine that it would turn out to be the monster success it has become. In 2008, a second Burger Bar opened in St. Louis, where, according to several accounts, burgers were invented at the 1904 St. Louis World's Fair. And now there is a third Burger Bar in San Francisco on Union Square.

We were in Las Vegas at the invitation of the Mandalay Bay casino to create a second Fleur de Lys. Laurent had joined us to become the chef of the new Fleur de Lys. A job he continued, even as he became essential to our work with Burger Bar. Construction delays gave Chantal, Laurent, and I time to consider what to do with another restaurant space in the casino's shopping plaza called Mandalay Place, a unique collection of restaurants and boutiques.

We wanted to create a place exciting enough to draw people to Mandalay Place. It should be inexpensive so that anyone could come. We knew everyone loves burgers, but we wanted to offer something new. What if we re-imagined burgers, and applied our fine-dining culinary expertise to create the best-tasting burgers possible? We would take them seriously because, we noticed, burger lovers take the subject seriously. Very seriously.

Although Laurent and I had little first-hand experience of American burger culture, we saw it as an advantage. We were not tied to any preconceived notions or traditions and quickly embarked on a whirlwind burger cram course. We read books and ate burgers from coast to coast and in every price range. Our ideas coalesced. We would start with the best quality meats, freshly ground every day. We would hand-shape each and every patty to ensure juiciness. But from there, we would leave it to the customer to choose.

Recognizing the need for the familiar as well as the desire for choice and surprise, we created a **build your own** menu for Burger Bar. Diners first choose their patty: three kinds of beef (all USDA prime), plus buffalo, turkey, fish, chicken, or veggie. Then a bun (five choices). Bacon? Choose apple smoked, black pepper, jalapeño, or cinnamon. Cheese? Eight choices, from cheddar to pepper Jack. And on to toppings, relishes, and condiments, from pesto to caramelized onions, sautéed mushrooms, Maine lobster, black truffles, and more.

For this book, I've expanded on the **build your own** idea. You will find a collection of succulent burgers organized by type of meat, poultry, fish, vegetarian, and even dessert. Photographs show them complete with my suggestions for sauces, buns, condiments, garnishes, and such. But as you build your burgers from the bun up, you will see that they can easily be disassembled and reassembled to suit your taste. You can pare the presentations down to the essentials or borrow a relish or accompaniment from one recipe to serve with another. The important thing is to cook, not to follow the recipe exactly. For example, I varied my selections of lettuces and greens to maximize color, flavor, and textural contrasts, but feel free to use any lettuce you have on hand.

I've included burgers appropriate for many different tastes, budgets, and occasions. For a weekday supper, when ease and speed are priorities, you might make the Black Jack Burger. We named it for the card game; the first Burger Bar is in a Las Vegas casino, after all. When getting together with friends on a Friday night over a good bottle of wine, make the Buffalo Burger. The lean, flavorful meat has become a great favorite at Burger Bar. For a brunch or supper dish, you might enjoy the novel presentation of a classic American comfort dish, Mac and Cheese Burgers. And for a weekend splurge, what could be more spectacular than a Fleur Burger showered with black truffles? (It's still less expensive than a fancy night out.)

As a Frenchman, I usually prefer a glass of red wine with meat. But when the menu focuses on burgers, more Americans opt for beer or milkshakes. When we opened Burger Bar, we decided to feature the largest beer selection on tap on the entire Las Vegas Strip. Since then, we've worked to develop our reserve list of specialty bottled beers. Customers like to try different burger-and-beer combinations. Feel free to do the same. A brief dsicussion of burger-and-beer matching is on page 162.

Great burgers begin with great ingredients prepared simply and well. That means the patties themselves—how the meat is ground, mixed, shaped, seasoned, and finally cooked. The following Building Better Burgers section gives you all the information you will need to do it yourself.

I hope you will expand on the **build-your-own** theme by finding inspiration in the ideas and flavor combinations I've presented, and then cooking according to your palate and purse, adding and subtracting components as you wish. So, come on, let's have fun and get cooking!

BUILDING BETTER BURGERS

Did American culture create the burger? Or did the burger engineer modern American culture?

Built to satisfy large hungers—for juice-dripping-down-the-chin deliciousness, for the sound of fat sizzling and jumping as it hits hot coals, for Meat spelled with a capital M, for adventure embodied in glossy, grazing cattle guarded by rugged cowboys—burgers occupy a large, vital territory in American food consciousness. Quintessentially democratic, burgers belong to everyone. Biting into a thick, succulent burger, we all feel rich.

Made of high-quality ingredients, flavored and accessorized with inventive condiments and sauces, and given innovative presentations, the burger is once again reinventing itself and the way Americans eat at home and in restaurants.

QUALITY MATTERS

Being obsessed with meat, its quality and handling, is the secret to a great burger. The meat must be mixed and shaped by hand. No machine yet exists that can do these steps and maintain the necessary light—you could even say airy, fluffy texture in the patty. The contrast between a well-tended burger's inner fluffiness and outer, well-browned crust provides the burger's unique flavor experience. Lose that texture and you sacrifice essential, juicy toothsomeness. The truth is in the taste.

Because we are obsessed with meat, Burger Bar offers meat and seafood from specialty producers. And each Burger Bar has its own butcher shop. Daily, we divide and trim large cuts and grind them. Then we hand-mix the meat to distribute the fat evenly throughout. The meat is weighed into 8-ounce portions and hand-shaped. Every one of the thousand burgers we sell on a typical Saturday in Las Vegas is made the same way.

At home, for burgers that deliver "This-is-the-best-burger-I-ever-tasted" flavor, choose the highest-quality ingredients. Your local specialty butcher and fish-monger are your greatest allies in your quest to produce the ultimate burger experience. They will offer the widest selection and the freshest meats and fish. Shop for meat from specific breeds and smaller producers, such as those raising organic and grass-fed animals for meat.

When selecting meat, choose prime or choice grades. Chuck, with its natural marbling, makes a delicious burger. When a beef burger calls for a better cut, such as the NY Strip Surprise Burger, you might go all the way and try dry-aged sirloin. Aging reduces the water content and concentrates the flavor of meat and fat. And American Kobe is especially rich and flavorful (see page 6). Look at the photo on page xii to see the texture and marbling differences.

Specialty butchers are also more likely to carry a broad range of ground meats, including buffalo and lamb, rare items just a few years ago. Buffalo, an incredibly lean (just 3 percent fat) meat, is enjoying increased popularity as its healthful properties and great, meaty taste become more widely recognized. Grass-fed meat, too, tends to be leaner than meat from animals fed grain. Ostrich might be mistaken for beef: Its flesh is quite red and also very lean. Your butcher can order it for you.

The shoulder cuts of lamb and pork (the pork shoulder is called the "butt"), with their mix of flavorful meat and fat, are the best choices for burgers. For chicken and turkey, make your burgers from the dark meat. It contains the most flavor and slightly more fat. Try to avoid prepackaged and pre-shaped burgers; freshly ground turkey and chicken will be moister and tastier.

Meaty-fleshed fish with robust flavors, such as tuna and salmon, lend themselves most easily to burgers. But the sweet succulence of crab and shrimp can make irresistible burgers. Just be sure your seafood is impeccably fresh.

BURGER BASICS

I confess that when I tested all of these burger recipes at home, I bought ground meat from quality butchers and had outstanding results. This is because shaping the patties contributes even more than grinding to a burger's flavor and texture. What you do not want to buy is meat stuffed and compacted into plastic packaging. Once the meat is compacted, a light texture cannot be regained. A good butcher gives you fine quality and plenty of choices.

There is a trend now to offer ground meats with varying amounts of fat. For the greatest juiciness and depth of flavor, shop for ground meat with 15 percent fat or more. However, adding other ingredients to the ground meat can compensate for very lean meat. For example, the Pesto Beef Burger has pesto kneaded into the patties for extra flavor and richness. The same rule applies to lean poultry and fish. You can add ingredients to preserve and increase juiciness. For instance, you might marinate chicken in coconut milk; or add sautéed onions, mushrooms, or other vegetables; or moisten the meat with a spoonful of olive oil or mayonnaise.

But for the ultimate burger, it's worthwhile grinding great-quality meat at home. There are three primary methods: chopping by hand; using a grinder, either an attachment to a stand mixer, for instance, or a hand-operated one; or pulsing in a food processor. My French training tells me that the very best steak tartare is always chopped by hand with a very sharp knife. First, the meat is cut into very thin slices. These are cut lengthwise into matchsticks, and then crosswise into a very tiny dice. The resulting texture is very light and fluffy. Hand-chopped meat and fish results in burgers with a delicate texture and extra juiciness.

However you grind the ingredients for your burgers, two rules apply: Have your meat cold, and make sure the cutting blade is very sharp. You want to cut the meat cleanly. Grinding can warm meat; when warm, it tends to compact easily; when cooked, compact patties are less juicy.

Maintain the loose, fluffy texture with gentle shaping. Work quickly and chill the

continues on page 6

Follow these tips for great burgers every time.

GRINDING MEAT

Because of the speed of the blade, the food processor will warm meat more than other modes of grinding. Put the work bowl and the blade in the freezer for 20 minutes before grinding. And have the meat very cold, just above freezing. If you use a hand grinder or a stand-mixer grinding attachment, you can also refrigerate or freeze these for 30 to 60 minutes before use.

Trim the cold meat, cutting out any large, solid pieces of fat. Then cut the meat into small pieces that can be easily fed into the grinder—larger pieces for grinders and about $1\frac{1}{2}$-inch cubes for the food processor.

Using your hands, lightly knead the ground meat to evenly distribute the fat. Chill the meat after grinding, or season the meat (omitting salt at this stage) and form it into patties. Then refrigerate again until you are ready to cook.

SHAPING PATTIES

Remove the meat from the refrigerator only when you are ready to shape the burger patties, and then refrigerate the patties as soon as you have shaped them. Handle the meat lightly enough to preserve its juiciness and lightness of texture, yet firmly enough that the patties hold their shape during cooking.

If the meat is to be seasoned before shaping—for instance, if you are adding onions, garlic, and spices—sprinkle the seasonings evenly over the chilled ground meat in a bowl. Mix the ingredients together with a light, quick kneading action. If you have time, chill the meat again before shaping to allow the flavors to meld.

At Burger Bar, to produce patties with a uniform diameter and thickness, we weigh portions and use a mold. At home you could weigh out portions if you like, but a quick way to achieve consistent size and weight would be to scoop the meat into a 1-cup measure or a ramekin.

Working with damp hands, gather the meat into a ball. On a work surface, rotate it quickly between your cupped palms, then lightly pat it down into a circle. Continue rotating and patting until you have an evenly round patty that fits your bun and is about an inch thick. As each patty is shaped, place it on a parchment-lined sheet pan. Put another sheet of parchment or waxed paper between layers of patties. Cover the whole with plastic wrap and refrigerate until needed.

For cooking on top of the stove and for grill grates, use well-seasoned cast iron. It can be preheated, without adding fat, until smoking hot. Its heavy weight allows it to distribute heat evenly as well as retain its heat even when filled with burger patties. Also, cast-iron pans go directly from the stove top into the oven, a decided plus if you like to finish your burgers in the oven.

Keep patties refrigerated until it is time to cook. If they are at room temperature, they may cook too quickly and lose their fat and thus their juiciness.

Season burgers right before cooking. And then season them generously with salt and pepper. If you salt them ahead of time, the salt tends to start curing the meat and can make it sweat and lose juiciness.

The most important rule: *Never press down on the patties.* You will only squeeze the juices out.

When cooking burgers on top of the stove, first brown them for a few minutes per side, then turn them once or twice more, if needed. Baste them with the fat in the pan. Turning allows the juices to move down into the meat, retaining its juiciness and promoting even cooking. Basting keeps the meat hot on top, also promoting even cooking.

On the other hand, too-frequent turning can compress the meat. Try this timing for stove-top cooking. Heat a tablespoon or two of olive oil in a large skillet over medium-high heat until very hot. Add the burgers and cook until brown on the first side, about 1 minute. Turn and brown the second side, about 3 minutes. Turn the meat again and baste several times with the juices in the pan while cooking for another 3 minutes for medium-rare burgers.

When cooking on a grill, to mark burgers or other foods—buns, for example—with even crosshatches, give them quarter turns at intervals of about $1\frac{1}{2}$ minutes. Too-frequent turning can result in uneven grill marks. Not moving the patties at all burns the grill marks too deeply in a single place.

Build a medium-hot fire in the grill. Brush the grate to clean it well and, once it's hot, oil it well. Place the burgers over direct heat. Cover the grill and cook for about $1\frac{1}{2}$ minutes. Give the burgers a quarter turn, re-cover the grill, and cook for another $1\frac{1}{2}$ minutes. Then turn the burgers over and repeat the process on the second side. About 7 minutes of cooking time should give you a medium-rare burger.

patties as soon as they are shaped. You can work well ahead, shaping the patties several hours or even a day ahead or even freezing the patties.

When ready to cook, for the best possible texture and flavor, quickly cook the burgers in a heavy, hot pan over medium-high heat or over a hot fire on a gas or charcoal grill. In my opinion, beef burgers taste best medium-rare. Especially if you cook American Kobe beef, with its rich marbling of fat, do not cook it past medium-rare. Its fat melts away in the pan or on the grill, resulting in a dry-tasting burger. The very lean buffalo and ostrich burgers, too, should be cooked just to medium-rare. Poultry and fish also should be cooked with a delicate hand so they are just cooked through but not overdone. Remember to let meat burgers rest for a couple of minutes before cutting or biting into them. The rest allows the meat to continue to cook very gently while the juices seep throughout the meat, ensuring a juicy eating experience.

A FEW NOTES ON SPECIAL INGREDIENTS

American-style Kobe Beef
This meat is amazingly tender and flavorful. To create this extravagant beef, American ranchers imported the Japanese cattle breed, Wagyu, which had been nurtured and developed around the city of Kobe. In America, Wagyu are often crossed with American breeds, especially the famous Black Angus. The American Wagyu cattle crosses take longer to mature than other breeds and are thus more expensive to raise. The best producers feed their animals well—a natural diet including barley and hay. They are not fed beer nor are the animals massaged as folk legend would have it.

American-produced Kobe beef provides a rich, complex beefy flavor, is beautifully marbled with fat, giving both tenderness and flavor, and is incredibly moist. If you compare side-by-side examples of American Kobe and Black Angus, for example, you can easily see the higher fat content and the looser texture of the Kobe.

While the meat is heavily marbled with fat, its ratio of monounsaturated fat over saturated fat is higher than that of commodity beef making the meat an arguably healthier choice. Because of this high fat content, American Kobe beef should be cooked carefully and not much beyond medium-rare or the fat will melt away. Then there is little flavor difference between it and a less-expensive beef.

Black Truffles

These are a miracle food, rare and precious. Botanically, they are the fruit of a fungus that grows underground on and around the roots of certain trees, especially oak trees. They are hunted by a handler with a specially-trained dog or pig. A good truffle dog is probably worth more than its weight in truffles.

During the winter harvest season truffles are found through their scent—they are headily aromatic. Then, the handler digs up each by hand. The best black truffles come from the Périgord region of France. They should be uniformly black, and smoothly knobbed. Inside, the flesh shows a tiny white netting of veins. The best and freshest black truffles have a strong, particular fragrance that combines fruitiness with the scent of forest undergrowth. The auction price for truffles averages between $850 and $1,500 per pound. Because of their expense, truffles are usually served in thin shavings scattered over foods. A little heat is all they need to release their fragrance.

Fleur de Sel

It is the most pure of the hand-harvested, naturally evaporated sea salts. It has a coarse, uneven texture and does not melt immediately upon contact with hot

QUICK CHICKEN STOCK

You can freshen and deepen the flavor of packaged stock and broth by cooking it slowly with aromatic vegetables and herbs. Use low-sodium or no-salt-added broth.

Put 2 quarts (8 cups) low-sodium chicken broth in a large pot with 1 roughly chopped yellow onion; 1 stalk celery, cut into chunks; 1 carrot, cut into chunks; 1 small leek, cut into chunks; 1 tomato, roughly chopped; and a crushed garlic clove. Add a sprig each of parsley and thyme and a bay leaf. Add about $\frac{1}{4}$ cup white wine or sherry.

Bring to a boil over high heat, then reduce the heat to a slow simmer and cook, uncovered, until reduced to about 6 cups, about 1 hour.

Strain, pressing down gently on the solids to extract as much liquid as possible. Discard the solids, and refrigerate the stock, covered, until needed.

foods. A sprinkle of it at the last minute before serving gives excitement and a pop of flavor, like a little explosion in the mouth.

Sea Salt
Throughout the book, when I call for salt, I mean sea salt. I find that it has a true salt flavor without added ingredients.

BUNS AND BREADS

Really, anything goes. A burger is, after all, a sandwich, so bread is an essential element. That said, you might keep in mind some general principles—as well as your own preferences—concerning texture, temperature, and taste.

If the burger and its fixings have an overall soft texture, you will want the bun to provide some contrast and crunch. Breads with a crisp but not too hard crust, like ciabatta, are a good choice. Toasting also gives a bun a crisper texture. Buns should, in my opinion, be warm. Warming freshens the bun flavor and helps keep the burger patty hot, too. Buns can be warmed in an oven, toasted in a toaster or under the broiler, or grilled on the perimeter of the grate.

To butter or not to butter: The choice, really, is an individual one. The burgers as presented have sauces, condiments, and plenty of natural juiciness to soak into the buns. But buns do toast more evenly and develop deeper, more attractive grill marks if they are buttered first. At Burger Bar, we brush the buns for savory burgers with butter. This adds an extra dimension of moistness and flavor.

You might also simply brush the buns with melted, unsalted butter or spread them with soft butter. Brushing the buns with herbed olive oil would be another easy way to add flavor to your burgers. When grilling, put a little pan of butter on the edge of the grill to melt. Then, you can give buns a quick swab with a silicone basting brush before putting them on the grill.

With so many artisan bakers and their products available across the country, you can now add flavor and flair to your burgers with your bun choice.

Try multigrain, whole wheat, potato, and seeded buns; olive, walnut, or even dark rye breads, thinly sliced and toasted; tortillas and pita bread; and English and corn muffins.

If your store does not carry a variety of burger buns, look at the selection of dinner rolls. These are often a good size for burgers, and you will be able to find rye, multigrain, sourdough, olive, and more.

Make buns from a larger loaf. For instance, you can make ciabatta buns by cutting a loaf into four or six squares and splitting these in half. Baguettes and focaccia also can be cut into buns.

For savory or sweet burgers, there are surprising and delicious choices including doughnuts, brioche, waffles, puff pastry, and cake and cookie batters cooked in individual molds such as English muffin rings.

BIG BEEF BURGERS

BIG BEEF BURGERS

BLACK JACK BURGER

We named this burger after the casino card game. We make it with Black Angus beef, Jack cheese, and a black condiment, tapenade, to underscore the name. But the flavor combination is more than just show business. The rich, salty pungency of the olive paste adds complexity to the burger's flavors.

SERVES 4

2 pounds coarsely ground chuck, chilled
2 tablespoons olive oil plus 1 teaspoon
Sea salt and freshly ground black pepper
4 slices (about 6 ounces) Monterey Jack cheese

4 ciabatta buns
About $1/_2$ cup Tapenade (page 128)
4 large leaves butter lettuce
1 medium, ripe tomato, thinly sliced

Handling lightly to keep the texture light and juicy, divide the meat into 4 evenly sized, thick patties. The burgers can be shaped and refrigerated, covered, for several hours or overnight.

When ready to cook, heat the olive oil in a large skillet or grill pan over medium-high heat until very hot or build a medium-hot fire in a barbecue. Generously season the meat on both sides with salt and pepper.

Cook the burgers in the skillet, turning once or twice, for 7 to 10 minutes for medium-rare. Do not press down on the patties. With a large spoon, baste the burgers several times with the fat in the pan. (You can also preheat the oven to 450°F and cook the burgers on top of the stove until they are brown on both sides, and then finish them in the oven.) To grill the burgers,

oil the grate, arrange the patties on it, and cover. Cook as above.

For the last minute or two of cooking, drape a slice of cheese over each burger to melt. Then remove them to a warm platter, keep warm, and let rest for several minutes before serving.

While the burgers cook, toast the buns in a toaster oven or under the broiler, about 5 inches from the heat, until lightly toasted. Or toast them on the outer perimeter of the grill rack.

To build the burgers, spread each of the bun bottoms with about a tablespoon of tapenade. Top with a lettuce leaf, and then with overlapping layers of tomato. Add the burgers, and then a generous dollop of tapenade. Cover with the bun tops. Serve immediately.

BLUE CHEESE-STUFFED BACON SLIDERS

A classic combination: blue cheese, bacon, and pear. But these burgers are inside out—the cheese hides inside the burgers. As the burgers cook, the cheese melts and bastes them. I've used sirloin, a more expensive cut than usual for burgers, but sliders make great party food when you want to splurge on ingredients. **Build your own:** You can also make the burgers with lamb. These proportions will make 8 large burgers. I've mixed bacon into the burgers and used it as a garnish, too. You can do either. Also, you can omit the grilled pear, or, if it's good and ripe, use it raw. Beet Pickles (page 113) make a great-tasting and colorful accompaniment.

SERVES 12

16 slices (1 pound) apple-smoked bacon

2 ripe but firm pears

About 1 tablespoon sugar

3 pounds coarsely ground sirloin, chilled

1 tablespoon finely chopped fresh thyme

Freshly ground black pepper

6 ounces (about $1/_2$ cup) crumbled blue cheese, at room temperature

2 tablespoons olive oil plus about 1 teaspoon

Sea salt

24 soft, mini burger buns

$2^1/_2$ cups baby arugula leaves

1 small red onion (about the same diameter as the buns), very thinly sliced

1 pint basket cherry tomatoes (optional)

In a large skillet over medium heat, cook the bacon until crispy, and then drain on paper towels. Cut 8 of the slices crosswise into 3 pieces each; crumble the remaining bacon and set both aside separately.

Peel the pears, halve them lengthwise, and core them. Cut them crosswise into thin slices and put in a bowl. Toss with the sugar and set aside.

In a large bowl, combine the meat, thyme, crumbled bacon, and $1/_2$ teaspoons pepper. Using your hands, knead together lightly. Form the mixture into 48 evenly sized balls (about 1 ounce each). Use the pointed end of an egg to make a small depression in half the patties. Fill them with a little mound of cheese, dividing it evenly among them. Top with the remaining patties, and then pinch them together around the cheese. Make sure the stuffing is completely enclosed. Pat and mold the burgers to fit the buns. The burgers can be shaped and refrigerated, covered, for several hours or overnight.

When ready to cook, heat 2 tablespoons of the olive oil in a large skillet over medium-high heat until very hot or build a medium-hot fire in a barbecue. Generously season the meat on both sides with salt and pepper.

Cook the burgers in the skillet, in batches, turning once or twice, about 3 minutes for medium-rare. Do not press down on the patties. Be gentle when you turn the burgers so they do not break open. With a large spoon, baste the sliders several times with the fat in the pan. To grill the burgers, oil the grate, arrange the patties on it, and cover. Cook as above.

While the burgers cook, toast the buns in a toaster oven or under the broiler, about 5 inches from the heat, until lightly toasted. Or toast them on the outer perimeter of the grill rack.

When the burgers are done, remove them to a warm platter, keep warm, and let rest for several minutes. Meanwhile, heat the remaining teaspoon of the olive oil in a nonstick skillet over medium heat and add the pear slices, or place them on the outside of the grill rack, and cook just until warm and lightly browned. Turn and repeat, then remove to a plate. They should still be crunchy.

To build the burgers, arrange a few leaves of arugula on the bun bottoms. Top each with a pear slice or two, a piece of bacon, and a burger. Add an onion slice and a bun top, and skewer securely together. Add a cherry tomato as a topknot, if you wish, on the skewer. Serve immediately.

BURGER AND FRIES

An all-in-one burger: Crisp, shredded potatoes encase the burger, forming a "bun." I like to serve this knife-and-fork burger with a deeply flavored red wine sauce. The potatoes soak up the sauce and turn into an addictively crunchy and savory taste experience. To make the burgers easier to handle, I suggest making 6-ounce burgers and letting them come to room temperature before starting to cook. Don't worry about soaking or rinsing the potatoes; they need to be sticky to properly adhere to the meat. They will release water once they have been cut, especially if cut ahead of time, so be sure to squeeze this excess water out before wrapping the burgers. Also, cook these burgers in a nonstick skillet. On a grill, I regret to report that the potato coating will fall off. **Build your own:** Use the potato coating for other burgers or even for steaks and chops.

SERVES 4

1½ pounds coarsely ground chuck, chilled
2½ pounds russet potatoes, peeled
Sea salt and freshly ground black pepper
1 large egg white, beaten

3 tablespoons olive oil, plus more as needed
1 handful baby greens or Fried Herbs (page 137)
½ pint basket cherry tomatoes, quartered
Red Wine, Thyme, and Shallot Sauce (page 136)

Handling lightly

to keep the texture light and juicy, divide the meat into 4 evenly sized patties about 1 inch thick. The burgers can be shaped and refrigerated, covered, for several hours or overnight. Let the meat come to room temperature before cooking.

With a mandoline, julienne the potatoes into the finest possible strips. Put them in a bowl and season with salt and pepper to taste. Toss to mix well.

When ready to cook, preheat the oven to 450°F.

Wrap the burger patties in potatoes only just before cooking. Brush the patties with the beaten egg white. Enclose the potatoes in a clean kitchen towel and press to rid them of excess water. Divide the potatoes into 8 equal piles. Spread one pile on a work surface, top with a patty, and then spread another pile of potatoes on top and all around the meat.

Gently but firmly press the potatoes around the meat, working the patty between your hands to form a tight package and to completely cover the meat with the potatoes.

Heat the olive oil in a large, ovenproof, nonstick skillet over medium-high heat until very hot. Place the burgers in the skillet and cook without moving them until the potatoes begin to turn golden brown and crisp, about 3 minutes. Regulate the heat to prevent burning.

Turn the burgers and place in the oven for 8 to 9 minutes for medium-rare. Add more oil to the skillet as needed so the potatoes do not stick or burn. (It might be helpful here to use a meat thermometer. It should register 125°F for medium-rare meat.)

To build the burgers, center the burgers on warm plates. Garnish with a pinch of baby greens or fried herbs. Scatter a few cherry tomatoes and greens around the burgers and serve immediately with the sauce on the side, or spoon a circle of sauce around the burgers.

PESTO BEEF BURGER

The elements of this burger are simplicity itself, but when added together they are more than the sum of their parts. The pesto gets mixed into the meat, adding juiciness and a terrific herbal flavor. Make sure to use a bun with a crunchy crust. You want the textural contrast. **Build your own:** Substitute a basil pesto or leave it out altogether. Try sautéed instead of grilled onions.

2 pounds coarsely ground chuck, chilled
Cilantro-Arugula Pesto (page 127)
Freshly ground black pepper
2 tablespoons olive oil
Sea salt
4 thick slices (about 6 ounces) provolone cheese

4 ciabatta buns
Grilled Onion Steaks (page 105)
1 large tomato, cut into 4 thick slices
Large handful arugula
Fleur de sel (optional)

In a bowl, mix together the meat, $\frac{1}{4}$ cup pesto, and $1\frac{1}{2}$ teaspoons pepper. Handling lightly to keep the texture light and juicy, divide the meat into 4 evenly sized, thick patties. The burgers can be shaped and refrigerated, covered, for several hours or overnight.

When ready to cook, heat the olive oil in a large skillet or grill pan over medium-high heat until very hot or build a medium-hot fire in a barbecue. Generously season the meat on both sides with salt and pepper.

Cook the burgers in the skillet, turning once or twice, for 7 to 10 minutes for medium-rare. Do not press down on the patties. With a large spoon, baste the burgers several times with the fat in the pan. (You can also preheat the oven to 450°F and cook the burgers on top of the stove until they are brown on both sides, and then finish them in the oven.) To grill the burgers, oil the grate, arrange the patties on it, and cover. Cook as above.

For the last minute or two of cooking, drape a slice of cheese over each burger to melt. Then remove them to a warm platter, keep warm, and let rest for several minutes before serving.

While the burgers cook, toast the buns in a toaster

oven or under the broiler, about 5 inches from the heat, until lightly toasted. Or toast them on the outer perimeter of the grill rack.

To build the burgers, spread the bun bottoms with about a tablespoon of the remaining pesto. Top with the tomato slices and then the arugula. Add the burgers and then a grilled onion on top of each. Sprinkle with fleur de sel, if using. Cover with the bun tops. Serve immediately with any remaining pesto on the side.

MUSHROOM BEEF BURGER

Mushroom lovers get a double hit with this burger. Grilled mushrooms mixed into the patties add a wonderful smokiness. Then more mushrooms are mixed into the mayonnaise to spread on the buns. If the mushrooms are young and fresh, you do not need to remove the gills from the underside of the mushroom caps. However, if they seem dry to you, scrape the gills away with a small knife. Cover the grill when cooking the mushrooms to increase the smoky flavor. You can even do this indoors by inverting a pie plate over the mushrooms for the last few minutes of cooking. **Build your own:** You could also use the mushrooms as a topping. To simplify the preparation, omit the asparagus. And try other cheeses such as Fontina or Gruyère.

SERVES 4

About $1/2$ cup olive oil
1 tablespoon plus $1/4$ teaspoon finely chopped fresh thyme
1 teaspoon freshly grated lemon zest
$1/2$ pound (about 5 medium) portobello mushrooms, stems removed
Sea salt and freshly ground black pepper
1 pound asparagus

2 pounds coarsely ground chuck, chilled
$1/2$ cup finely chopped red onion
1 tablespoon Dijon mustard
$1/2$ cup mayonnaise
4 ciabatta buns
4 large slices (about 6 ounces) Brie cheese
1 large ripe tomato, thickly sliced

In a shallow container, whisk together 3 tablespoons of the olive oil, 1 tablespoon of the thyme, and the lemon zest. Add the mushrooms and turn to coat them on all sides. Set aside to marinate for about 30 minutes. The mushrooms will absorb all the marinade.

To prepare the asparagus, bring a pot of water to a boil and add salt. Trim the spears to an even 4-inch length. If the skin is tough, peel the bottom 2 inches of the stalks. Blanch the asparagus in the boiling water for about 2 minutes, drain, and spread out on a baking sheet to cool. Toss with a little olive oil and season with salt and pepper. Set aside.

Build a medium-hot fire in a barbecue or place a grill pan over medium-high heat. Grill the mushrooms, turning as needed, and brushing with a little olive oil if they seem dry, until they are well browned and tender, about 10 minutes. Remove to a chopping board, let cool, and cut them into small dice.

In a large bowl, combine the meat with two-thirds of the mushrooms, the onion, mustard, and $1\frac{1}{2}$ teaspoons pepper. Knead gently until the ingredients are evenly mixed. Handling lightly to keep the texture light and juicy, divide the meat into 4 evenly sized patties about 1 inch thick. The burgers can be shaped and refrigerated, covered, for several hours or overnight.

In a small bowl, mix together the remaining mushrooms with the remaining $\frac{1}{4}$ teaspoon thyme and the mayonnaise. Cover and set aside.

When ready to cook, heat 2 more tablespoons of the olive oil in a large skillet or grill pan over medium-high heat until very hot or build a medium-hot fire in a barbecue. Generously season the meat on both sides with salt and pepper.

Cook the burgers in the skillet, turning once or twice, for 7 to 10 minutes for medium-rare. Do not press down on the patties. With a large spoon, baste the burgers several times with the fat in the pan. (You can also preheat the oven to 450°F and cook the burgers

on top of the stove until they are brown on both sides, and then finish them in the oven.) To grill the burgers, oil the grate, arrange the patties on it, and cover. Cook as above.

While the burgers cook, toast the buns in a toaster oven or under the broiler, about 5 inches from the heat, until lightly toasted. Or toast them on the outer perimeter of the grill rack.

For the last minute or two of cooking, drape a slice of cheese over each burger to melt. Then remove them to a warm platter, keep warm, and let rest for several minutes before serving.

To reheat the asparagus, in another large skillet, heat 1 tablespoon olive oil over medium-high heat until hot. Add the asparagus and cook, turning often, until tender and lightly browned, about 3 minutes. You can also reheat the spears on the grill, turning them frequently.

To build the burgers, spread each bun bottom with about a tablespoon of the mushroom mayonnaise. Arrange several asparagus spears on the bun bottoms, then the tomato slices, and then the burgers. Add another dollop of mushroom mayonnaise. Cover with the bun tops and serve immediately.

SURF AND TURF BURGER

This succulent tower pairs Black Angus beef with Maine lobster. It's a feast and a very popular burger at Burger Bar. **Build your own:** Make it for a Saturday-night dinner party and cook the lobster yourself and include all the garnishes. For a barbecue, you might want to streamline the burger and do without all the garnishes. And, if you want to concentrate on lobster alone, simply pile it on a bun with asparagus and mayo. You'll have a swell time.

Many aspects of the recipe can be completed ahead of time and need only a quick reheating just before serving. You can cook this dish indoors or out, but it is easier on the grill because the lobster, asparagus, and pineapple cook alongside the beef. Use a grill insert that allows easy handling of small items.

SERVES 4

1 pound asparagus
About 5 tablespoons olive oil
Sea salt and freshly ground black pepper
2 pounds coarsely ground sirloin, chilled
2 small cooked lobster tails, halved lengthwise
4 soft buns
4 thin slices ripe pineapple, peeled
About $1/4$ cup Green Peppercorn and
   Lemon Mayonnaise (page 126)
1 teaspoon sugar
2 large, ripe tomatoes, thinly sliced
Fleur de sel (optional)
Handful baby greens or sprouts

To prepare the asparagus,

bring a pot of water to a boil and add salt. Trim the spears to an even 4-inch length. If the skin is tough, peel the bottom 2 inches of the stalks. Blanch the asparagus in the boiling water for about 2 minutes, drain, and spread out on a baking sheet to cool. Toss with a little olive oil and season with salt and pepper. Set aside.

Handling lightly to keep the texture light and juicy, divide the meat into 4 evenly sized patties about 1 inch

thick. The burgers can be shaped and refrigerated, covered, for several hours or overnight.

Preheat the oven to 375°F to reheat the lobster.

When ready to cook, heat 2 tablespoons of the olive oil in a large skillet or grill pan over medium-high heat until very hot or build a medium-hot fire in a barbecue. Generously season the meat on both sides with salt and pepper.

Cook the burgers in the skillet, turning once or twice, for 7 to 10 minutes for medium-rare. Do not press down on the patties. With a large spoon, baste the burgers several times with the fat in the pan. (You can also preheat the oven to 450°F and cook the burgers on top of the stove until they are brown on both sides, and then finish them in the oven.) To grill the burgers, oil the grate, arrange the patties on it, and cover. Cook as above. Remove them to a warm platter, keep warm, and let rest for several minutes before serving.

While the burgers cook, toast the buns in a toaster oven or under the broiler, about 5 inches from the heat, until lightly toasted. Or, toast them on the outer perimeter of the grill rack. Brush both sides of each bun with some of the mayonnaise and arrange on 4 warmed plates.

While the burgers cook, prepare the pineapple and reheat the asparagus. Heat 1 tablespoon of the olive oil in a large skillet over medium-high heat until quite hot. Add the pineapple. Cook, turning occasionally, until almost soft, about 3 minutes. Sprinkle half the

sugar over the pineapple, turn, and cook until light gold. Sprinkle on the remaining sugar, turn, and cook until golden. Keep warm. To grill the pineapple, toss it with 1 tablespoon olive oil and arrange it on the grill, away from direct heat. Cook until light brown on one side, then turn and brown the second side. Sprinkle it lightly with sugar and cook, turning once or twice, for another minute or so. Be careful that the slices do not burn.

To reheat the asparagus, in another large skillet, heat 1 tablespoon olive oil over medium-high heat until hot. Add the asparagus and cook, turning often, until tender and lightly browned, about 3 minutes. Or toss the asparagus with 1 tablespoon olive oil and arrange on the grill with the pineapple. Cook, turning the spears carefully, until lightly browned all over, about 2 minutes. Keep hot.

To reheat the lobster, use the remaining 1 tablespoon olive oil to brush the lobster pieces and to film a skillet with oil. Season the lobster with salt and pepper. Arrange the lobster in the pan and place it in the preheated oven to warm, about 5 minutes, while building the burger. Or brush the lobster with olive oil, season with salt and pepper, and place on the grill away from direct heat. Cook gently just to reheat.

To build the burgers, arrange the asparagus on the bun bottoms and then the tomato slices. Add the burgers and pineapple, and balance a half lobster tail on top. Sprinkle with fleur de sel, if using, and garnish the burgers with a pinch of baby greens. Arrange the bun tops against the burgers. Serve immediately and pass the remaining mayonnaise at the table.

BURGER AU POIVRE

This recipe turns a classic French preparation for skirt or New York strip steak into a burger. Here, I have mimicked the shape of the steak by forming the ground meat into oblong burgers, which fit neatly into buns cut from baguettes. The peppercorn blend tweaks the traditional blend by adding whole coriander seeds. **Build your own:** Use the peppercorn blend for everyday cooking. If you prefer, you can also buy a multi-pepper blend in the supermarket. Make the burgers round to fit a soft bun or serve open-face on crunchy toast. I recommend cooking these burgers on top of the stove; otherwise the peppercorns might fall off and burn.

SERVES 4

1 tablespoon dried whole green peppercorns
1 tablespoon whole white peppercorns
1 tablespoon whole pink peppercorns
1 tablespoon whole black peppercorns
1 tablespoon whole coriander seeds
2 pounds coarsely ground New York strip steak
  or sirloin, chilled
About $\frac{1}{2}$ cup Dijon mustard
2 tablespoons olive oil
Sea salt

1 tablespoon cognac or brandy
$\frac{1}{4}$ cup dry red wine
$1\frac{1}{2}$ cups Quick Chicken Stock (page 7) or
  packaged low-sodium chicken broth
2 tablespoons heavy cream
1 large baguette, cut into 4 buns, each about
  5 inches long
2 large handfuls salad mix
2 small ripe tomatoes, thinly sliced

In a small bowl, mix together the green, white, pink, and black peppercorns with the coriander. Enclose the mix in a clean kitchen towel and, with the edge of a heavy pan or the flat side of a meat tenderizer, crush the peppercorns. You want fairly large, crunchy pieces, not a powder. Shake the mixture into a small bowl.

Handling gently to keep the texture light and juicy, divide the meat into 4 evenly sized, elongated patties about 1 inch thick. Generously brush the patties on both sides with the mustard, reserving 1 teaspoon. Then press about $1\frac{1}{2}$ teaspoons cracked pepper onto the top and bottom of each patty. The burgers can be shaped and refrigerated, covered, for several hours or overnight.

When ready to cook, heat the olive oil in a large skillet over medium-high heat until very hot. Generously season the meat on both sides with salt.

Cook the burgers in the skillet, turning once or twice, for 7 to 10 minutes for medium-rare. Do not press down on the patties. With a large spoon, baste the burgers several times with the fat in the pan. (You can also preheat the oven to 450°F and cook the burgers on top of the stove until they are brown on both sides, and then finish them in the oven.) Remove the burgers to a warm platter and keep warm while making the pan sauce.

Pour off the fat remaining in the skillet and return it to medium-high heat. Add the cognac and the red wine and stir and scrape all over the bottom and sides of the pan to loosen all the browned bits. Cook until the pan is nearly dry, about 2 minutes, and then add the stock. Bring to a boil and cook until reduced by half, about 3 minutes. Add the cream and simmer to meld the flavors, another 3 to 4 minutes. Stir in the remaining teaspoon mustard and immediately remove the pan from the heat. You should have about 2 tablespoons of sauce per person.

While the sauce reduces, toast the buns in a toaster oven or under the broiler, about 5 inches from the heat, until lightly toasted.

To build the burgers, moisten the bun bottoms with a little of the sauce. Top with the salad mix, tomatoes, and then the burgers. Pour the remaining sauce over the burgers and cover with the bun tops. Serve immediately.

BLACK AND BLUE BURGER

These burgers are based on the French bistro dish steak tartare. In the classic dish, a nest of raw meat is presented with a raw egg in the center and the condiments arranged around the edge of the plate. Here, the tartare ingredients are kneaded into the meat. The patties are then seared very well on the outside but remain very rare ("blue") inside.

Be sure to buy meat from a trusted source. Have the meat at room temperature, otherwise it may remain cold in the center when the outside has properly seared. Make sure to serve crisp buns to provide a textural contrast to the burgers. **Build your own:** If concerned about undercooked meat, simply cook the burgers to your desired doneness. You can also omit the poached egg and fried herb garnish.

SERVES 4

1 1/2 pounds coarsely ground sirloin, chilled
2 tablespoons finely chopped red onion
1 tablespoon capers, drained and roughly chopped
1 tablespoon finely chopped cornichons
1 tablespoon finely chopped fresh flat-leaf parsley
3 tablespoons mayonnaise
3 tablespoons Dijon mustard, either smooth or coarse-grained
1 tablespoon plus 1 1/2 teaspoons finely chopped fresh tarragon or cilantro

4 large eggs
2 tablespoons white wine vinegar
Sea salt and freshly ground black pepper
2 tablespoons olive oil
4 ciabatta buns
1 large heirloom tomato, thinly sliced
2 large handfuls salad mix
Fried Herbs (optional; page 137)
Fleur de sel

In a large bowl, use your hands to gently knead the meat together with the onion, capers, cornichons, parsley, 2 tablespoons of the mayonnaise, and 1 tablespoon of the mustard. Handling lightly to keep the texture light and juicy, divide the meat into 4 evenly sized patties about 1 inch thick. Let rest for 30 minutes at room temperature.

In a small bowl, mix together the remaining 2 tablespoons mustard with the remaining 1 tablespoon mayonnaise and the tarragon. Set aside.

To poach the eggs, fill a broad pan such as a sauté pan with $1\frac{1}{2}$ inches of water. Place over medium heat and bring to a very gentle simmer. Regulate the heat to keep the water barely simmering. Add the vinegar. Break an egg into a small heatproof cup and lower it slowly into the water. Tip the egg into the water; the white should immediately collect around the yolk. Repeat for the other 3 eggs. Cook just until the whites are set and the yolks are soft,

about 90 seconds. Drain the eggs on paper towels. Keep warm.

Generously season the burgers on both sides with salt and pepper. Heat a large, heavy skillet over high heat until very, very hot. Add the oil and immediately add the burgers. Cook them until just brown on one side, about 1 minute. Immediately turn them over to cook on the second side until just brown, about $1\frac{1}{2}$ minutes. Transfer the burgers to a warm plate.

While the burgers cook, toast the buns in a toaster oven or under the broiler, about 5 inches from the heat, until lightly toasted.

To build the burgers, brush the bun, tops and bottoms, with the mustard-mayonnaise mixture. On the bun bottoms, arrange the tomatoes, salad mix, burgers, poached eggs, and a pinch of the fried herbs, if using. Sprinkle a little fleur de sel over the burgers. Prop the bun tops against the burgers and serve immediately.

THE NEW YORK STRIP SURPRISE BURGER

The burger credited with starting it all—the so-called "gourmet" burger trend—was New York City chef Daniel Boulud's DB Burger luxuriously stuffed with braised short ribs and foie gras. This recipe is my adaptation of that original idea. It might be labor-intensive but makes a fantastic burger. To braise well requires patience; you cannot hurry slow-cooked dishes. But they require very little tending, and, once complete, you can refrigerate the meat or even freeze it. So make plenty and you'll be able to quickly put together these elegant, dinner-party-quality burgers, plus a hearty pasta dish with the leftovers.

SERVES 4

Braised Short Ribs

2 pounds meaty, bone-in short ribs
1 tablespoon olive oil
Sea salt and freshly ground black pepper
$^1/_2$ cup roughly chopped yellow onion
$^1/_4$ cup roughly chopped carrot
$^1/_4$ cup roughly chopped celery
2 garlic cloves, finely chopped

1 cup dry red wine
1 bay leaf
2 teaspoons finely chopped fresh thyme
$^1/_2$ teaspoon ground coriander
1 tomato, cut into 6 wedges
3 cups Quick Chicken Stock (page 7) or packaged
　low-sodium chicken or beef broth

Short Rib–Stuffed Burgers

$^1/_2$ pound shredded Braised Short Ribs
3 tablespoons finely chopped fresh chives
$1^1/_2$ pounds coarsely ground New York strip steak,
　chilled
2 tablespoons olive oil, plus more for brushing
Sea salt and freshly ground black pepper

4 ciabatta buns
About $^1/_2$ cup reserved braising liquid
4 slices (about 6 ounces) Gruyère cheese
4 large leaves butter lettuce
1 large heirloom tomato, thinly sliced

To make the short ribs: In a sauté pan or Dutch oven, heat the olive oil over medium-high heat until very hot. Season the meat well with salt and pepper and brown it all over, about 10 minutes. Remove the meat to a plate and discard all but about 1 tablespoon of the fat in the pan.

Add the onion to the pan, stir well, and cook over medium heat until it has softened and taken on some color, about 5 minutes. Add the carrot, celery, and garlic and cook until all the vegetables have colored, about 5 minutes. Add the wine and bring to a boil over high heat while stirring and scraping all over the sides and bottom of the pan. Return the meat to the pan with the bay leaf, thyme, coriander, and tomato. Cook until the wine is reduced by half. Add the stock—it should come at least halfway up the height of the meat—and bring just to a boil. Cover and simmer very slowly until the meat is so tender it falls off the bone, 2 to 3 hours. Check the liquid level occasionally and add stock or water if needed to keep the level about 1 inch deep. Let the meat cool in the braising liquid for about 1 hour. (To oven-braise, bring the mixture to a boil on top of the stove and then place in a preheated 300°F oven for about 3 hours.)

Pick out the meat, shred it into a bowl, cover, and refrigerate. Strain the braising liquid into another bowl, cover, and refrigerate. When the fat has risen to the top and solidified, remove and discard it. If you have more than 1 cup braising liquid, pour it into a saucepan and bring it to a boil over medium-high heat. Cook until the liquid is reduced to 1 cup. Dip the bottom of the pan in cold water to stop the cooking.

Pour about $1/4$ cup of the sauce into the shredded meat and toss until well combined. Reserve the remaining sauce separately. The recipe can be completed to this point 1 to 2 days ahead of time. Or you can freeze the meat and sauce separately.

To make the burgers: Let the

short ribs come to room temperature. Place them in a bowl and toss with the chives. Handling lightly to keep the texture light and juicy, divide the ground beef into 8 evenly sized patties. Arrange about 2 tablespoons of short ribs in the center of each of 4 patties. Top with the remaining 4 patties and pinch the edges closed to seal the meat around the stuffing. Pat and shape into patties about 1 inch thick. Cover and refrigerate for at least 1 hour to meld the flavors, or for as long as overnight. Remove the prepared patties 30 minutes before cooking.

When ready to cook, heat 2 tablespoons of the olive oil in a large skillet over medium-high heat until very hot or build a medium-hot fire in a barbecue. Season the meat on both sides with salt and pepper.

Cook the burgers in the skillet, turning once or twice, for 7 to 10 minutes for medium-rare. Do not press down on the patties. With a large spoon, baste the burgers several times with the fat in the pan. (You can also preheat the oven to 450°F and cook the burgers on top of the stove until they are brown on both sides, and then finish them in the oven.) To grill, oil the grate, arrange the patties on it, cover, cook as above.

While the burgers cook, brush the buns with olive oil and toast them in a toaster oven or under the broiler, about 5 inches from the heat, until lightly toasted. Or toast them on the outer perimeter of the grill rack. Reheat the reserved braising liquid over low heat.

For the last minute or two of cooking, drape a slice of cheese over each burger to melt. Then remove them to a warm platter, keep warm, and let rest for several minutes while dressing the buns.

To build the burgers, moisten the bun bottoms with a little of the braising liquid. Arrange the lettuce and tomato slices on each. Place the burgers on top, cover with the bun tops, and serve immediately. Serve the remaining sauce on the side as a dip for fries.

FLEUR BURGER WITH TRUFFLES

When you order a FleurBurger 5000, you hit the gastronomic jackpot: the ultimate burger-and-wine pairing experience. The burger, made with American Kobe beef, black truffles, and a rich, aromatic wine sauce, comes with a bottle of 1990 Château Pétrus, a wine that itself is redolent of truffles. The burger is an interpretation of a classic Escoffier preparation—filet mignon served on a crouton and topped with foie gras and truffles. **Build your own:** For the home version, I've omitted the foie gras and added bright red pickled onion. Its tart taste makes a good foil for the rich meat and sauce. In place of the truffle, try other wild mushrooms. And choose whatever wine you like.

SERVES 4

2 pounds coarsely ground American Kobe beef, chilled
1 teaspoon cornstarch
1 cup Quick Chicken Stock (page 7) or packaged low-sodium chicken broth
2 tablespoons olive oil
Sea salt and freshly ground black pepper
2 tablespoons ruby port

4 brioche buns
3 tablespoons unsalted butter, at room temperature
1 ounce black truffle, very thinly sliced, about 5 slices per serving (optional)
4 handfuls baby greens or sprouts
Grenadine Pickled Onions (page 134)
Fleur de sel

To make the burgers, shape the meat into 4 evenly sized patties about 1 inch thick. Handle lightly to keep the texture light and juicy. The burgers can be shaped and refrigerated, covered, for several hours or overnight.

When ready to cook, in a small bowl stir together the cornstarch and about 2 tablespoons of the stock until well blended. Set aside.

Heat the olive oil in a large skillet or grill pan over medium-high heat until very hot. Generously season the meat on both sides with salt and pepper.

Cook the burgers in the skillet, turning once or twice, for 7 to 10 minutes for medium-rare. Do not press down on the patties. With a large spoon, baste the burgers several times with the fat in the pan. (You can also preheat the oven to 450°F and cook the burgers on top of the stove until they are brown on both sides, and then finish them in the oven.) Remove the burgers to a warm platter and reserve the cooking skillet. Keep the burgers warm, and let rest for several minutes before serving.

Working quickly so the burger skillet is still hot, pour out any remaining fat and return the pan to medium-high heat. Add the port and stir and scrape all over the sides and bottom of the pan to dislodge all the browned bits. Add the remaining stock and bring to a boil. Cook until reduced by about a third, about 2 minutes. Add the cornstarch mixture and cook and stir until the sauce has thickened, about 1 minute.

Toast the buns in a toaster oven or under the broiler, about 5 inches from the heat, until lightly toasted. Or toast them on the outer perimeter of the grill pan. Use 2 tablespoons of the butter to spread on the cut sides of the buns. Set aside.

Heat the remaining 1 tablespoon of butter in a small skillet over medium heat until the butter begins to bubble. Add the truffle slices, if using, and cook, stirring and tossing, until the truffles are warm through, about 30 seconds. Set aside and keep warm.

To build the burgers, arrange a small handful of greens on the bun bottoms and spread a spoonful of pickled onions on the greens. Put the burgers on top and divide the truffle slices evenly among them. Lightly drizzle the sauce over and around the burgers, and then sprinkle with fleur de sel. Balance the bun tops against the burgers and serve immediately.

MORE MEATY BURGERS

BUFFALO BURGER

This is a simple and great-tasting cheeseburger. The meat has a deep, rich flavor and is becoming more popular as people come to understand that buffalo is healthful as well as delicious. The red wine–cooked onions add complexity and moistness to the buffalo. **Build your own:** You could omit the onion (in that case, be extra careful not to overcook the burger), use them for a topping, or knead them into a beef or lamb burger. If pressed for time, use raw apple for its sweet-tart crunch or leave it out. Tapenade (page 128) would make a great addition to this burger, adding rich, pungent flavor and moisture.

SERVES 4

2 tablespoons unsalted butter
$1/_2$ medium (about $2^1/_2$ ounces) red onion, finely chopped
$1/_2$ cup dry red wine
1 teaspoon finely chopped fresh thyme
2 pounds coarsely ground buffalo, chilled
Freshly ground black pepper
2 tablespoons olive oil

Sea salt
1 large, unpeeled tart apple, cored and cut into $1/_4$-inch-thick rounds
About 2 tablespoons brown sugar for sprinkling
4 focaccia buns
4 slices (about 6 ounces) Gruyère cheese
2 large handfuls watercress and/or sprouts
1 large, ripe tomato, thinly sliced (optional)

In a medium sauté pan, melt 1 tablespoon of the butter over medium heat. Add the onion and stir and cook until translucent, about 5 minutes. Add the wine and thyme, bring to a boil, and cook until the pan is nearly dry, about 10 minutes. Let the onion cool to at least room temperature. The onion can be cooked a day ahead, covered, and refrigerated.

Using your hands, gently knead the meat in a large bowl together with the onion and $1\frac{1}{2}$ teaspoons pepper. Handling lightly to keep the texture light and juicy, divide the meat into 4 evenly sized patties about 1 inch thick. The burgers can be shaped and refrigerated, covered, for several hours or overnight.

When ready to cook, heat the olive oil in a large skillet or grill pan over medium-high heat until very hot or build a medium-hot fire in a barbecue. Generously season the meat on both sides with salt and pepper.

Cook the burgers in the skillet, turning once or twice, for 7 to 10 minutes for medium-rare. Do not press down on the patties. With a large spoon, baste the burgers several times with the fat in the pan. (You can also preheat the oven to 450°F and cook the burgers on top of the stove until they are brown on both sides, and then finish them in the oven.) To grill the burgers, oil the grate, arrange the patties on it, and cover. Cook as above.

While the burgers cook, melt the remaining 1 tablespoon butter and brush the apple slices on both sides. Place them in a sauté pan over medium heat or on the perimeter of the grill to cook slowly. You want them to get tender but not fall apart. After about 1 minute, turn the slices and sprinkle them lightly with brown sugar. Cook for another minute, turn, and sprinkle with sugar again. Turn, cook for another minute, and then immediately remove the slices to a plate. Cut the slices in half.

When the burgers are about half cooked, toast the buns in a toaster oven or under the broiler, about 5 inches from the heat, until lightly toasted. Or toast them on the outer perimeter of the grill rack.

For the last minute or two of cooking, drape a slice of cheese over each burger to melt. Then remove them to a warm platter, sprinkle with pepper, keep warm, and let rest for several minutes before serving.

To build the burgers, fan apple slices on the bun bottoms, and top with watercress, tomato slices, if using, burgers, and then the bun tops. Serve immediately.

FEIJOADA BURGER

My experience living in Brazil inspired this pork burger. It deconstructs *feijoada*, the Brazilian national dish of black beans and assorted meats, a simple description of a dish that can take days to prepare. **Build your own:** For the best flavor, cook the black beans yourself. And while you are at it, make extra. Scoop out 2 cups worth, drain them well, and use them for the Southwestern Bean Burger on page 93. You can, of course, use canned beans.

SERVES 4

Black Beans

3 cups broth such as vegetable broth or
   chicken stock or water
$^2/_3$ cup dried black beans, picked over and rinsed
3 tablespoons roughly chopped yellow onion
1 strip (about 1 ounce) bacon, cut into small pieces
2 tablespoons roughly chopped celery

1 tablespoon freshly grated orange zest
$1^1/_2$ teaspoons finely chopped fresh thyme
1 teaspoon finely chopped garlic
1 teaspoon finely chopped peeled fresh ginger
1 bay leaf
Sea salt and freshly ground black pepper

Pork Burgers

1 teaspoon whole coriander seeds
1 teaspoon whole cumin seeds
2 pounds coarsely ground pork butt, chilled
2 teaspoons finely chopped peeled fresh ginger
1 teaspoon freshly ground black pepper plus more
   for seasoning
1 jalapeño, seeded and finely chopped
2 tablespoons olive oil
Sea salt

4 soft buns, preferably slightly sweet and milky,
   such as Portuguese bread
1 medium sweet yellow onion such as Maui, thinly
   sliced and separated into rings
Small handful cilantro leaves
1 large orange, peeled, and sliced into rounds
About 1 cup Brazilian Pickled Vegetables (page 111)
1 handful sprouts or baby salad mix (optional)

To make the beans:
In a medium saucepan, combine the broth, beans, onion, bacon, celery, orange zest, thyme, garlic, ginger, and bay leaf. Bring to a simmer, cover, and cook until the beans are tender and you have a thick, stew-like consistency, about 1 hour. Discard the bay leaf. Mash the beans lightly with a potato masher just to break them up. Season to taste with salt and pepper. Keep warm.

To make the burgers:
In a small, dry pan, toast the coriander and cumin seeds over medium-low heat until they are fragrant and lightly browned, about 2 minutes. Pour onto a small plate to cool, and then grind to a powder.

Using your hands, gently knead the meat in a large bowl together with the ground coriander and cumin, ginger, 1 teaspoon of pepper, and jalapeño. Handling lightly to keep the texture light and juicy, divide the meat into 4 evenly sized patties about 1 inch thick. The burgers can be shaped and refrigerated, covered, for several hours or overnight.

When ready to cook, heat the olive oil in a large skillet or grill pan over medium-high heat until very hot or build a medium-hot fire in a barbecue. Generously season the meat on both sides with salt and pepper.

Cook the burgers in the skillet, turning once or twice, for about 7 minutes on each side for medium. Do not press down on the patties. With a large spoon, baste the burgers several times with the fat in the pan. (You can also preheat the oven to 450°F and cook the burgers on top of the stove until they are brown on both sides, and then finish them in the oven.) To grill the burgers, oil the grate, arrange the patties on it, and cover. Cook for 5 to 7 minutes per side for medium.

While the burgers cook, toast the buns in a toaster oven or under the broiler, about 5 inches from the heat, until lightly toasted. Or toast them on the outer perimeter of the grill rack.

To build the burgers, moisten the bun bottoms with a spoonful of beans, then add a few onion rings and a few cilantro leaves. Add the burgers, and then arrange the orange slices on top. Add a tuft of sprouts, if using. Cover with the bun tops. Serve with small bowls of the pickled vegetables and the beans on each plate.

PROVENÇAL BURGER

These crowd-pleasing burgers are packed with the zesty flavors of the south of France. The relish, with roasted pepper and tomato, enhances the Mediterranean tastes. **Build your own:** You can do without the relish and the burgers themselves will still be a delicious experience. You could also add Tapenade (page 128) or use it instead of the relish. All the preparations can be completed ahead of time, leaving you with just burgers to flip at mealtime.

SERVES 4

1 teaspoon whole coriander seeds, lightly crushed
1 teaspoon whole cumin seeds, lightly crushed
$1/4$ cup dry red wine
1 tablespoon honey
2 pounds trimmed, coarsely ground lamb (preferably from the shoulder), chilled
2 teaspoons minced garlic
$1/4$ cup (about $1/2$ small) finely chopped red onion

Freshly ground black pepper
2 tablespoons olive oil
Sea salt
4 ciabatta buns
4 leaves butter lettuce
About 1 cup Spicy Red Pepper–Tomato Relish (optional; page 130)

In a small, dry pan, toast the coriander and cumin over medium-low heat until they are lightly browned and fragrant, about 2 minutes. Stir in the wine and honey. Bring to a boil over high heat and cook until reduced by about half. Set aside to cool to room temperature.

Place the lamb in a large bowl and add the garlic,

onion, and toasted spice–wine mixture. Season with $1/2$ teaspoons pepper and knead together lightly but thoroughly. Handling lightly to keep the texture light and juicy, divide the lamb into 4 evenly sized patties about 1 inch thick. Cover and refrigerate for at least 30 minutes or as long as overnight.

When ready to cook, heat the olive oil in a large

skillet or grill pan over medium-high heat until very hot or build a medium-hot fire in a barbecue. Generously season the meat on both sides with salt and pepper.

Cook the burgers in the skillet, turning once or twice, for 7 to 10 minutes for medium-rare. Do not press down on the patties. With a large spoon, baste the burgers several times with the fat in the pan. (You can also preheat the oven to 450°F and cook the burgers on top of the stove until they are brown on both sides, and then finish them in the oven.) To grill the burgers, oil the grate, arrange the patties on it, and cover. Cook as above.

While the burgers cook, toast the buns in a toaster oven or under the broiler, about 5 inches from the heat, until lightly toasted. Or toast them on the outer perimeter of the grill rack.

When the burgers are done, remove them to a warm platter, keep warm, and let rest for several minutes while dressing the buns.

To build the burgers, arrange a lettuce leaf on the bun bottoms. Add a spoonful of the pepper-tomato relish, if using, and place the burgers on top. Spoon more relish on the side of each plate and on top of the burgers. Cover with the bun tops and serve immediately.

GREEK BURGER

A buffet of sun-drenched Greek flavors in a single burger. There's crunch, color, tang, and herbal and olive flavors combined with the succulent richness of lamb and grilled eggplant. For this burger, I've mixed lamb and beef, which gives a rich, complex flavor. **Build your own:** When pressed for time, serve simply grilled eggplant instead of the marinated eggplant or leave it out. You could use all lamb or all beef for the burgers.

$1\frac{1}{3}$ pounds coarsely ground lamb shoulder, chilled

$\frac{2}{3}$ pound coarsely ground chuck, chilled

2 garlic cloves, very finely chopped

1 tablespoon finely chopped fresh oregano

1 tablespoon freshly grated lemon zest

$1\frac{1}{2}$ teaspoons sweet paprika

Sea salt and freshly ground black pepper

Olive oil for brushing

Marinated Eggplant (page 108) or 1 large (about 1 pound) purple eggplant sliced

4 ciabatta buns

About $\frac{1}{3}$ cup Tapenade (page 128)

1 small English cucumber, halved, seeded, and cut crosswise into crescents

1 large tomato, thinly sliced

2 ounces (about $\frac{1}{3}$ cup) crumbled feta cheese

Handful baby greens

Place the lamb and beef in a large bowl and add the garlic, oregano, lemon zest, paprika, and 1 teaspoon of pepper. Knead the ingredients together lightly but thoroughly. Handling lightly to keep the texture light and juicy, shape the lamb into 4 evenly sized patties about 1 inch thick. Cover and refrigerate for at least 30 minutes or as long as overnight.

If using fresh eggplant, cut it into $\frac{1}{2}$-inch thick rounds, sprinkle them lightly on both sides with salt, and leave in a colander to drain for about 30 minutes. Rinse and then dry throroughly by pressing between sheets of paper twoels or tea towels. Brush the slices on both sides with olive oil and set aside.

When ready to cook, build a medium-hot fire in a barbecue. Generously season the meat on both sides with salt and pepper and brush with olive oil. Oil the grate, arrange the patties on it, cover, and cook, turning once or twice, for 7 to 10 minutes for medium-rare. When the burgers are done, remove them to a warm platter, keep warm, and let rest for several minutes.

While the burgers cook, reheat the marinated eggplant on the perimeter of the grill or place the eggplant slices on the grill, and cook until browned on both sides and tender throughout, about 8 minutes. When the burgers are about half done, toast the buns on the outer perimeter of the grill rack.

To build the burgers, spread a generous tablespoon of tapenade on each bun bottom. Add a bed of cucumber, then tomato slices, burgers, and a slice or two of eggplant. Sprinkle the cheese over the burgers and top with a pinch of baby greens. Cover with the bun tops and serve immediately.

BREAKFAST BURGER

This little "burger" is a quiche without the crust. It makes a fun and savory weekend breakfast or brunch. The batter can be mixed together the night before. For baking, use silicone egg cups or jumbo muffin molds. **Build your own:** Since it is a quiche, you can vary the filling to reflect the season, for instance, melted leek with mushrooms, or assorted contents from your refrigerator.

SERVES 4

12 large fresh basil leaves
3 large eggs
$\frac{1}{2}$ cup whole milk
$\frac{1}{4}$ cup heavy cream
5 tablespoons freshly grated Parmesan cheese
Pinch of freshly grated nutmeg
3 tablespoons finely chopped fresh
   flat-leaf parsley
$\frac{1}{4}$ pound ham, cut into thin strips

Sea salt and freshly ground black pepper
About 2 tablespoons unsalted butter
4 English muffins
1 ripe avocado, pitted, peeled, very thinly sliced
4 large leaves butter lettuce
1 ripe tomato, preferably heirloom, cut into wedges
1 teaspoon minced shallot
4 slices prosciutto
Fruit Fries (page 120)

Preheat the oven to 375°F.

Stack the basil leaves in 2 piles. Fold them in half along their spines, and then cut crosswise into very thin strips. Set aside.

In a mixing bowl, whisk together the eggs, milk, cream, Parmesan, and nutmeg. Add the basil, parsley, ham,

and a pinch of salt and pepper. Go easy on the salt, as the ham provides salt.

Melt about $\frac{1}{2}$ teaspoon butter in each of 4 oven-proof egg cups and arrange them on a baking sheet. Divide the egg mixture evenly among the cups. Bake them until golden brown on top, about 15 minutes. The burgers will puff up during baking and then deflate when they come out of the oven.

While the burgers are baking, toast the muffins, butter both sides with the remaining butter, and keep warm. Fan out the avocado slices on the cutting board and divide them into 4 portions.

To build the burgers, arrange a lettuce leaf on each muffin bottom. Top with tomatoes, sprinkle with shallots, season with salt and pepper, and then unmold the burgers onto the tomatoes. Top each with a small fan of avocado and then a prosciutto slice. Cover with the muffin tops and serve with a small bowl of the fruit fries on the side.

BURGERS ON THE WING

MUSTARD SEED CHICKEN BURGER

The secret to this chicken burger bursting with flavor is mustard seeds. They are soaked until they pop easily against the teeth, like the best caviar but with a spicy hit. **Build your own:** Serve the burger with the Spicy Red Pepper-Tomato Relish (page 130) instead of the Endive-Apple Salad or try sliced raw apple for a change. The soaked mustard seeds keep very well in the refrigerator and give an extra zap of flavor to mashed potatoes, soups, pasta, and roasted fish, and to cream and butter sauces.

SERVES 4

3 tablespoons dry white wine

2 tablespoons brown mustard seeds

1 tablespoon white wine vinegar

1 tart green apple, peeled

$1\frac{1}{2}$ pounds uncooked, skinless, boneless, dark chicken meat (from legs and thighs), coarsely chopped and chilled

1 tablespoon Dijon mustard

4 green onions, white and light green parts only, finely sliced (about $\frac{1}{2}$ cup)

2 tablespoons olive oil, plus more for brushing

Sea salt and freshly ground black pepper

4 onion buns

1 ripe avocado

Piquillo Pepper Ketchup (page 132)

Endive-Apple Salad (page 122)

In a small saucepan, mix together the wine, mustard seeds, and vinegar. Bring to a boil and pour into a small bowl. Cover and let sit at room temperature overnight. The seeds will soften and swell. Drain and reserve the seeds. Refrigerate in a covered container until needed. The mustard seeds can be soaked and drained well ahead of time.

Coarsely shred the apple into a large bowl. Add the chicken, mustard seeds, Dijon mustard, and green onions. Lightly but thoroughly knead them together well. Handling lightly to keep the texture light and juicy, divide the chicken into 4 evenly sized patties about 1 inch thick. Cover and refrigerate for at least 30 minutes or as long as overnight.

When ready to cook, heat 2 tablespoons of the olive oil in a large skillet or grill pan over medium-high heat until very hot or build a medium-hot fire in a barbecue. Brush the burgers on both sides with olive oil and generously season on both sides with salt and pepper.

Cook the burgers in the skillet, turning once or twice, until browned and cooked through, 10 to 15 minutes. Do not press down on the patties. With a large spoon, baste the burgers several times with the fat in the pan. (You can also preheat the oven to 450°F and cook the burgers on top of the stove until they are brown on both sides, and then finish them in the oven.) To grill the burgers, oil the grate, arrange the patties on it, and cover. Cook until done as above.

While the burgers cook, toast the buns in a toaster oven or under the broiler, about 5 inches from the heat, until lightly toasted. Or toast them on the outer perimeter of the grill rack.

When the burgers are done, remove them to a warm platter, keep warm, and let rest for several minutes while dressing the buns. Peel, pit and slice the avocado.

To build the burgers, spread the bun bottoms with the ketchup. Add several avocado slices, then sprinkle the burgers with salt and pepper. Top with a small pile of the endive-apple salad. Cover with the bun tops and serve immediately. Pass more of the ketchup at the table.

OPEN-FACED CHICKEN BURGER

Here's a delicious, juicy chicken burger that combines uptown and downtown flavors: the smoky notes of barbecue in the chicken and the sophisticated succulence of the butter topping that melts into a rich sauce with the heat of the burger. The patties are delicate and are easiest to cook in a nonstick pan. Serve with Heirloom Cherry Tomato Salad (page 117). **Build your own:** The burger can stand on its own with just ketchup and/or mustard. If you have some Old-Fashioned Mustard (page 129) or Piquillo Pepper Ketchup (page 132) on hand, so much the better.

SERVES 4

$1\frac{1}{2}$ pounds coarsely ground, skinless, boneless dark chicken meat (from legs and thighs), chilled

1 large egg, lightly beaten

2 tablespoons barbecue sauce

2 tablespoons finely chopped fresh flat-leaf parsley

2 tablespoons olive oil, plus more for brushing

Sea salt and freshly ground black pepper

4 slices crusty bread, such as olive bread

4 tablespoons Tapenade (optional; page 128)

2 large handfuls arugula or salad mix

4 generous tablespoons Shallot-Tarragon Butter (page 135)

In a large bowl, gently and thoroughly knead together the chicken, egg, barbecue sauce, and parsley, and egg. Handling delicately, gently shape the chicken into 4 evenly sized patties about 1 inch thick. Cover and refrigerate for at least 30 minutes or as long as overnight.

When ready to cook, heat 2 tablespoons of the olive oil in a large, nonstick skillet over medium-high heat until very hot. Brush the burgers on both sides with olive oil and generously season them on both sides with salt and pepper.

Cook the burgers in the skillet, turning once or twice, until browned and cooked through, 10 to 15 minutes. Regulate the heat so they cook through without burning. Do not press down on the patties. With a large spoon, baste the burgers several times with the

fat in the pan. (You can also preheat the oven to 450°F and cook the burgers on top of the stove until they are brown on both sides, and then finish them in the oven.)

While the burgers cook, brush both sides of the bread with olive oil and toast the slices in a toaster oven or under the broiler, about 5 inches from the heat.

When the burgers are done, remove them to a warm platter, keep warm, and let rest for several minutes while dressing the toasts.

To build the burgers, spread the toast with tapenade, if using. Add arugula or salad, burgers, and a generous spoonful of the shallot butter. Serve immediately so the butter has not completely melted by the time the burgers arrive at the table.

BLT TURKEY CLUB BURGER

The best American bacon, lettuce, and tomato sandwich celebrates the return of summer's heirloom tomatoes to local markets. Crisp toast, juicy and aromatic turkey burgers, and a garlicky mayonnaise turn it into a three-decker extravaganza. Serve the burgers with Panisse Fries (page 102), with more of the aïoli for dipping. **Build your own:** Make the sandwich a single-decker; use an herb-flavored mayonnaise or simply plain mayonnaise.

SERVES 4

$1/_4$ pound (about 1 large link) uncooked hot Italian pork sausage, chilled
$1 1/_4$ pounds ground turkey, chilled
2 garlic cloves, finely chopped
$1/_2$ teaspoon ground cumin
Salt and freshly ground black pepper
8 strips bacon, halved crosswise

1 loaf rustic bread, as thinly sliced as possible
About $1/_2$ cup Spicy Aïoli (page 125)
2 large handfuls salad mix
2 large tomatoes, preferably heirloom, thinly sliced

Remove the casing from the sausage and crumble it into a large bowl. Add the turkey, garlic, and cumin. Season with $3/_4$ teaspoon of pepper and knead together lightly but thoroughly.

Handling lightly to keep the texture light and juicy, divide the turkey into eight 3-ounce patties about $1/_3$ inch thick. Cover and refrigerate for at least 30 minutes or as long as overnight.

Put the bacon in a large skillet and place it over medium heat. Cook the bacon until crispy, about 5 minutes. Drain the bacon on paper towels and set aside. Pour off all but 2 tablespoons of bacon fat from the skillet and set the skillet aside.

When ready to cook, return the skillet with the bacon fat to medium-high heat until very hot or

build a medium-hot fire in a barbecue. Generously season the meat on both sides with salt and pepper.

Cook the burgers in the skillet, turning once or twice, until browned and cooked through but still juicy, about 7 minutes. Do not press down on the patties. With a large spoon, baste the burgers several times with the fat in the pan. (You can also preheat the oven to 450°F and cook the burgers on top of the stove until they are brown on both sides, and then finish them in the oven.) To grill the burgers, oil the grate and brush the burgers on both sides with olive oil or reserved bacon fat from the skillet. Arrange the patties on it, cover, and cook as above.

While the burgers cook, toast the bread. You will need 3 slices per person. Toast them under the broiler, about 5 inches from the heat, until lightly toasted. Or grill the bread on the outer perimeter of the grill rack.

When the burgers are done, remove them to a warm platter, keep warm, and let rest for several minutes.

To build the burgers, spread the toast lightly on one side with the aïoli. Divide the salad mix among 8 of the slices, then top with tomato slices and 1 or 2 pieces of bacon. Add the burgers and stack 4 of the assembled burgers on the other 4, close with the remaining toast (aïoli side down), and secure with toothpicks.

OSTRICH BACON BURGER

As people continue to get more adventurous in their eating, new products are being discovered. Or, rediscovered. Ostrich is a very lean red meat. It has a great flavor but can dry out if overdone, so treat it as you would a beef burger and cook it just to medium-rare. I've added grilled onions to the patties to add moisture, and the bacon bastes them while they cook. Ground ostrich can be special ordered from quality butcher shops. **Build your own:** You may substitute duck if you like. Use the bacon-wrap idea with other lean burgers such as the buffalo, turkey, and even seafood patties. Top the burgers with thinly sliced raw onion and omit the vegetable relish.

SERVES 4

1½ pounds coarsely ground, skinless, boneless ostrich, chilled
½ recipe (about 1 cup) Grilled Onion Steaks, finely chopped (page 105)
8 strips bacon or slices pancetta
2 tablespoons olive oil
Sea salt and freshly ground black pepper

4 slices (about 6 ounces) cheddar cheese
4 soft buns
¼ cup Cilantro-Arugula Pesto (optional; page 127)
1 large ripe tomato, thinly sliced
4 leaves butter lettuce
Fleur de sel
Marinated Vegetable Salad (page 116)

In a large bowl, lightly but thoroughly knead together the ostrich and onions. Handling lightly to keep the texture light and juicy, divide the meat into 4 evenly sized patties about 1 inch thick. Wrap each patty in 2 strips of bacon. Cover and refrigerate for at least 30 minutes or as long as overnight.

When ready to cook, heat the olive oil in a large skillet or grill pan over medium-high heat until very hot

or build a medium-hot fire in a barbecue. Generously season the meat on both sides with pepper and only a little salt. The bacon will add salt, too.

Cook the burgers in the skillet, turning once or twice, until browned and cooked through, 7 to 10 minutes for medium-rare. Do not press down on the patties. With a large spoon, baste the burgers several times with the fat in the pan. (You can also pre-

heat the oven to 450°F and cook the burgers on top of the stove until they are brown on both sides, and then finish them in the oven.) To grill the burgers, oil the grate, arrange the patties on it, and cover. Cook as above.

For the last minute or two of cooking, drape a slice of cheese over each burger to melt. Then remove to a warm platter, keep warm, and let rest for several minutes before serving.

While the burgers cook, toast the buns in a toaster oven or under the broiler, about 5 inches from the heat, until lightly toasted. Or toast them on the outer perimeter of the grill rack.

To build the burgers, spread each bun bottom with pesto, if using. Add tomato slices, lettuce, burgers, and a sprinkle of fleur de sel. Cover with the bun tops and serve immediately with a spoonful of the vegetable salad on the side.

BURGERS FROM THE SEA

FROM THE SEA

SEARED TUNA BURGER

When the substantial, meaty texture of ahi tuna meets fresh ginger and toasted sesame oil, the result is a succulent, aromatic burger. Sesame vinaigrette flavors the patties themselves as well as the accompanying spinach salad. **Build your own:** You can also use yellowfin tuna instead of the ahi suggested here. It will be a lighter color but tastes great. You can use the vinaigrette for other green vegetables, such as broccoli and green beans, and serve them as room-temperature salads.

SERVES 4

Sesame Vinaigrette

1 garlic clove
1 slice peeled ginger, cut $\frac{1}{2}$ inch thick
$\frac{1}{4}$ cup mayonnaise
2 tablespoons toasted sesame oil

1 tablespoon freshly squeezed lime juice
1 tablespoon soy sauce
1 tablespoon unseasoned rice vinegar or
   cider vinegar

Tuna Burgers

1 large shallot
1 $\frac{3}{4}$ pounds ahi tuna, very cold and cut
   into 1-inch cubes
2 tablespoons chopped fresh cilantro
2 tablespoons Sesame Vinaigrette

Salt and freshly ground black pepper
2 tablespoons olive oil, plus more for brushing
4 sesame seed buns
4 handfuls baby spinach

To make the vinaigrette: Put the garlic and ginger in the bowl of a food processor and process until finely chopped. Add the mayonnaise, sesame oil, lime juice, soy sauce, and vinegar and process until well blended. Scrape the vinaigrette into a bowl and set aside until needed. Makes about $\frac{1}{2}$ cup.

To make the burgers: In the same work bowl of the food processor, process the shallot until finely chopped. Add the fish and pulse until roughly chopped.

Scrape the fish into a large bowl and add the cilantro,

the 2 tablespoons of vinaigrette, and 1½ teaspoons of pepper. Gently knead the ingredients together until evenly mixed. Using your hands, shape the fish into 4 evenly sized burgers about 1 inch thick. Cover and refrigerate for at least 30 minutes or as long as several hours to allow the flavors to develop.

When ready to cook, heat 2 tablespoons of the olive oil in a large skillet or grill pan over medium-high heat until very hot or build a medium-hot fire in a barbecue. Brush the burgers on both sides with olive oil and season well with salt and pepper.

Cook the burgers, turning once or twice, until golden brown on both sides, about 5 minutes. Take care not to overcook them. They should be rare to medium-rare. To grill the burgers, oil the rack, and cook the burgers, covered, about 5 minutes, turning once.

As the burgers cook, toast the buns in a toaster oven or under the broiler, about 5 inches from the heat, until lightly toasted. Or toast them on the outer perimeter of the grill rack.

To build the burgers, in a medium bowl, toss the spinach with half the reserved vinaigrette. Divide the spinach among the bun bottoms. Top with a burger and then spoon a little more vinaigrette on top. Cover with the tops of the buns and serve immediately.

DOUBLE SALMON TARTARE BURGER

In this recipe, I've combined fresh and smoked salmon with traditional steak tartare ingredients. The sharp, pickled, and savory flavors of the tartare mix add complexity and moistness to the burgers. **Build your own:** Use less smoked salmon or even leave it out, increasing the amount of fillet proportionately. You can also substitute smoked trout for the smoked salmon, or even white fish or sea scallops. The silky, flavorful mayonnaise-style dressing makes a terrific all-purpose sauce that goes very well with beef, chicken, and turkey burgers and is a great dip for french fries. And yes, I do mean four egg yolks in the dressing. They give the sauce an amazing richness. You can cut it down to two yolks and use the same amount of oil. These burger patties are somewhat fragile. If you grill them, do so on a grate meant for cooking delicate items.

SERVES 4

Tartare Dressing

4 large egg yolks
2 tablespoons ketchup
1 tablespoon Dijon mustard
2 teaspoons hot sauce, such as Tabasco

Sea salt and freshly ground black pepper
1 cup olive oil
3 tablespoons Worcestershire sauce

Salmon Burgers

1 medium shallot
1 heaping tablespoon capers, drained
2 cornichons
3 large sprigs fresh tarragon
5 sprigs fresh flat-leaf parsley
14 ounces skinless salmon fillet, chilled
6 ounces smoked salmon, chilled

2 tablespoons Tartare Dressing
1 unpeeled tart green apple
1 teaspoon freshly squeezed lemon juice
2 tablespoons olive oil
Sea salt and freshly ground black pepper
8 slices dark rye bread or rolls
2 to 3 large handfuls watercress

To make the dressing: In a food processor put the egg yolks, ketchup, mustard, hot sauce, and a good pinch of salt. Turn on the machine and begin adding the oil, at first drop by drop, increasing to a slow stream as the mixture forms an emulsion. Pulse in the Worcestershire sauce and salt and pepper to taste. Scrape the dressing into a bowl, cover, and refrigerate until needed. The sauce can be made a day ahead and refrigerated. Makes about 1$\frac{1}{2}$ cups.

To make the burgers: Put the shallot, capers, cornichons, parsley, and tarragon in the work bowl of a food processor and process until finely chopped. Cut the fish into cubes, add them to the work bowl, and chop with quick pulses, scraping down the sides as necessary. Stop when you still have texture; you want to chop the fish, not purée it. Pulse in the 2 tablespoons of dressing and $\frac{3}{4}$ teaspoon of pepper.

Shape the mixture into 4 evenly sized patties about 1 inch thick. Wrap well and refrigerate for at least 30 minutes to let the flavors develop or as long as several hours before cooking.

Halve and core the apple. Cut the halves crosswise into very thin slices. Toss them in a bowl with the lemon juice to prevent discoloration and set aside until needed.

When ready to cook, heat the olive oil in a large, heavy skillet or grill pan over medium-high heat until very hot or build a medium-hot fire in a barbecue. Generously season the burgers on both sides with salt and pepper. Cook until golden brown on both sides, turning once or twice, about 5 minutes total. To grill, oil the grate, and cook the burgers, covered, turning once, about 5 minutes. The burgers should have a nice crust but still be moist and barely cooked on the inside.

As the burgers cook, toast the bread in a toaster oven or under the broiler, about 5 inches from the heat. Or toast the slices on the outer perimeter of the grill rack.

To build the burgers, spread the toast with some of the tartare dressing. Fan a few slices of apple on 4 slices of the toast. Top with a tuft of watercress and then the burgers. Spoon a little of the remaining dressing onto the side of each plate, cover burgers with the remaining toast, and serve immediately.

SALMON FILLET BURGER

Make this exciting burger to showcase wild salmon. It's a classic combination of rich fresh fish, simply prepared, and cool, creamy cucumbers. Sometimes, I think, a cookbook becomes valuable for a single recipe or idea. Perhaps this is that idea: The burger is, very simply, a different presentation for fillet. It takes advantage of salmon's "stickiness." When the pieces of fish are bound together and cooked, they hold their shape. **Build your own:** Serve the shaped salmon patties on their own as the centerpiece of a formal dinner party menu.

SERVES 4

2 tablespoons olive oil, plus more for brushing
1 skinless salmon fillet (about 20 ounces), in a
    single piece
Sea salt and freshly ground black pepper
4 sesame seed buns
1 large tomato, thinly sliced

1 red onion, very thinly sliced
2 handfuls watercress
4 thin slices smoked salmon (optional)
Creamy Cucumber Salad (page 115)
2 tablespoons thinly sliced radishes (optional)
Soaked mustard seeds (optional; page 129)

Cut four 15 by 8-inch sheets of aluminum foil. Fold them in half lengthwise. Fold lengthwise twice more to make 15 by 1-inch strips. Brush the strips with oil.

With tweezers, remove any bones from the fillet. Cut the fillet crosswise into eight 1-inch-wide strips. They will be thicker in the middle and taper to each end.

To shape a burger, turn 2 slices up on their edge. Pull the tapered ends toward each other, "skin" side in, to form a U shape. Fit the 2 slices together, interlocking the Us. Gently pat them into a round. Wrap a foil strip, oiled side in toward the fish, around each fish burger like a belt. Twist the ends to firm the fillets into shape. Repeat to shape the remaining patties. The patties can be shaped in the afternoon, covered, and refrigerated until needed.

When ready to cook, heat the 2 tablespoons of olive oil in a large skillet or grill pan over medium-high heat until very hot or build a medium-hot fire in a barbecue. Brush the burgers on both sides with olive oil and season generously with salt and pepper. Cook until golden brown on both sides and cooked through, about 5 minutes total. Baste the burgers occasionally with the oil in the pan. To grill, oil the grate, and cook the burgers, covered, for about 5 minutes. Be careful not to overcook or the burgers will be dry. They should remain a little translucent in the center.

While the burgers cook, toast the buns in a toaster oven or under the broiler, about 5 inches from the heat, until lightly toasted. Or toast them on the outer perimeter of the grill rack.

To build the burgers, put the bun bottoms on warm plates. Layer on the sliced tomato and red onion, and then the watercress. Put the burgers on top and carefully unbelt them. Curl a slice of smoked salmon, if using, on top of the burgers and add a spoonful of cucumber salad. Top with a pinch each of radishes and mustard seeds, if using. Prop the top buns against the burgers, and serve immediately. Pass the remaining cucumber salad at the table.

BRAZILIAN ROCK SHRIMP BURGER

Rock shrimp make great burgers. They have a natural sweetness, that balances the addition of unusual flavors. Plus they have the helpful quality of natural binding. You do not need to add egg, bread crumbs, or other binding agents. Emphasize the exotic by serving lotus root gaufrettes (page 98) on the side. **Build your own:** Rock shrimp have a very hard shell, thus their name, and are sold already shelled. Do not substitute regular shrimp—however, chicken with these flavorings makes a great burger. These patties are delicate, so cook them in a nonstick pan or on a grill rack designed to cook delicate items.

SERVES 4

$^1\!/_3$-inch piece peeled fresh ginger

1 garlic clove

2 tablespoons plus 1$^1\!/_2$ teaspoons unsweetened
    coconut milk

Sea salt and freshly ground black pepper

1$^1\!/_2$ pounds rock shrimp, chilled

1 tablespoon finely chopped fresh cilantro

2 tablespoons olive oil, plus more for brushing

8 slices brioche bread

About $^1\!/_4$ cup mayonnaise (optional)

4 to 8 slices ripe tomato, preferably
    in different colors

2 handfuls salad mix

Grilled Avocado-Mango Salsa (page 119)

Place the ginger and garlic in a food processor and process until finely chopped. Add the coconut milk, 2 teaspoons of salt, and $^1\!/_2$ teaspoon of pepper and pulse to combine. Add the shrimp and cilantro and pulse until well chopped and the mixture is just shy of a purée. Make sure to leave some texture; do not purée.

To shape the burgers, use wet hands since the patty mixture is sticky. Handling lightly to keep the texture light and juicy, shape the shrimp into 4 evenly sized burgers about 1 inch thick. Cover and chill for at least 30 minutes to let the flavors develop or as long as several hours.

When ready to cook, heat 2 tablespoons of olive oil in a large, nonstick skillet over medium-high heat until very hot or build a medium-hot fire in a barbecue. Brush the burgers on both sides with olive oil and season generously with salt and pepper. Cook until golden brown and cooked through, about 8 minutes total. Regulate the heat as needed so the burgers can cook without burning. To grill, oil the grate, and cook the burgers, covered, as above. Be careful not to overcook or the burgers will be dry.

While the burgers cook, toast the bread in a toaster oven or under the broiler, about 5 inches from the heat, until lightly toasted. Or toast the slices on the outer perimeter of the grill rack. Brush the toast with mayonnaise, if using.

To build the burgers, arrange the tomatoes and salad mix on 4 pieces of toast, top with the burgers, and then spoon a little salsa on top. Cover with the remaining toast and serve immediately with the remaining salsa on the side.

CRAB SLIDERS

These delicious little burgers are a variation on crab cakes. Scallop mousse binds together the nuggets of fresh crab. The result is a burger with a more intense and complex seafood flavor. The light licorice flavor of fennel tastes wonderful with crab, so I've created a simple Marinated Fennel Salad (page 114) to serve with the sliders. You can use the fennel fronds to garnish the serving plate. You make the mousse in a blender or in a food processor, so it's done in a flash. I would not recommend grilling these on an outdoor barbecue because they are delicate and easily overcooked. **Build your own:** Serve the burgers without buns and garnishes as an appetizer.

SERVES 6

$\frac{1}{4}$ pound fresh sea scallops, chilled

1 large egg

Sea salt and freshly ground black pepper

$\frac{1}{2}$ cup heavy cream

1 pound fresh jumbo lump crabmeat, well drained and chilled

2 tablespoons finely diced red bell pepper

1 tablespoon Dijon mustard

1 tablespoon finely chopped fresh cilantro (optional)

Several drops of hot sauce, such as Tabasco

$\frac{1}{3}$ cup mayonnaise

2 teaspoons finely chopped fresh fennel fronds or tarragon

2 tablespoons olive oil, plus more as needed

12 soft, mini burger buns

2 handfuls greens, such as watercress or baby arugula

2 small, ripe tomatoes, thinly sliced

Marinated Fennel Salad (page 114)

Put the scallops and egg in a blender or food processor and process until well blended. Add 1 teaspoon of salt and a pinch of pepper. Pulse and process until the mixture is very thick and tight, like a stiff mayonnaise. With the machine running, add the cream very slowly in a steady stream until it is incorporated. You should have a scallop mousse with the texture of a thick mayonnaise. Scrape the mousse into a large bowl.

Make sure the crab is well drained; squeeze it between your hands to rid it of any excess moisture. Fold it into the scallop mousse with the red pepper, cilantro, mustard, and 3 drops of hot sauce until evenly mixed. Adjust the seasoning with salt, pepper, and more hot sauce, if desired. Refrigerate for 1 hour to let the mixture firm up a bit.

Using damp hands and handling the mixture lightly, shape the crab mixture into small burgers to fit the buns. (There is enough to make about twelve 1½-inch burgers.) Refrigerate for at least 15 minutes before cooking.

In a small bowl, mix the mayonnaise with a few drops of hot sauce to taste and the fennel fronds. Cover and set aside until needed.

When ready to cook, heat 2 tablespoons of olive oil in a large, nonstick skillet over medium-high heat until very hot. Generously season the burgers on both sides with salt and pepper. Cook until golden brown on both sides and cooked through, about 3 minutes total. Be careful not to overcook or the burgers will be dry. Add more oil if the burgers begin to stick to the pan.

While the burgers cook, toast the buns in a toaster oven or under the broiler, about 5 inches from the heat, until lightly toasted. Lightly spread the flavored mayonnaise onto the bun tops and bottoms.

To build the burgers, layer the greens, burgers, tomatoes, and a topknot of fennel salad on the bun bottoms. Cover with the bun tops and skewer together, if desired. Serve immediately, with any remaining fennel salad on the side.

BURGERS FROM THE GARDEN

MAC AND CHEESE BURGER

Comfort food transformed into an elegant burger: It's terrific for a weekend brunch or as a company supper dish or appetizer. I've made this rich version of macaroni and cheese on television in the past because it comes out of the oven with such a handsome brown glaze on top. It's rich and soul satisfying. **Build your own:** If you want to really gild the lily, add some poached lobster cut into large chunks to the macaroni mixture. The individual brioches, with fluted bottoms and browned topknots, make a great presentation. You can substitute other rolls made from a sweet, eggy yeast dough, such as challah.

SERVES 4

Sea salt and freshly ground black pepper
8 ounces elbow macaroni or small pasta shells
1 tablespoon unsalted butter
$\frac{1}{3}$ cup plus 2 teaspoons finely chopped shallot
$\frac{1}{4}$ cup finely chopped carrot
$\frac{1}{4}$ cup finely chopped celery
1 bay leaf
1 teaspoon finely chopped fresh flat-leaf parsley
1 teaspoon finely chopped fresh thyme
$1\frac{2}{3}$ cups heavy cream or half-and-half
2 tablespoons ruby port

1 tablespoon cognac or brandy
4 individual brioches à tête
2 tablespoons pine nuts
1 large egg yolk
3 tablespoons freshly grated Gruyère cheese
3 tablespoons extra-virgin olive oil
1 tablespoon freshly squeezed lemon juice
1 garlic clove, very finely chopped
4 large handfuls frisée lettuce or baby greens
4 radishes, thinly sliced
Small handful sprouts (optional)

Bring a large pot of water to a boil and add salt. Add the macaroni and cook, stirring occasionally, until tender, about 8 minutes. Drain and set aside.

In a large saucepan, melt the butter over medium heat. Add $\frac{1}{3}$ cup of the shallot, the carrot, celery, bay leaf, parsley, thyme, and salt and pepper to taste. Cook, stirring, until the vegetables have softened, about 5 minutes. Add 1½ cups of the cream, the port, and cognac. Bring to a simmer and cook, uncovered, until the mixture has thickened slightly, about 7 minutes.

While the cream sauce is cooking, hollow out the brioches. Leaving a rim of about ⅓ inch around the top, with a small, sharp knife cut down into the brioches and pull off the tops. Trim the lids and hollow out the brioches by carefully pulling out more of the insides. Lightly toast the hollowed-out brioches and their lids in a toaster oven or under the broiler, about 5 inches from the heat. They should just have a little crunchy texture when done; be careful not to burn them. Set aside and keep warm.

Preheat the broiler if it is not already on. In a dry pan over medium heat, toast the pine nuts until evenly brown, about 3 minutes. Immediately pour them onto a small dish to cool. In a small bowl, whisk the remaining cream with the egg yolk and set aside.

Stir the reserved macaroni and the cheese into the warm sauce. Spoon the mixture into the prepared brioches and set them on a baking sheet. Pour the yolk mixture over each stuffed brioche and broil until lightly browned, about 5 minutes.

While the stuffed brioches cook, make the salad. In a large bowl whisk together the extra-virgin olive oil, lemon juice, garlic, the remaining 2 teaspoons of shallots, and salt and pepper to taste. Add the lettuce and radishes and toss well with the dressing.

To build the burgers, divide the salad evenly among 4 plates and scatter the pine nuts on top. Arrange a stuffed brioche on each plate, add a pinch of sprouts, if using, and cover with the brioche tops.

ROASTED SQUASH–QUINOA BURGER

Great fall flavors season this delicious and healthy burger. I have always been interested in vegetarian dishes and have created many vegetarian menus for my restaurants. Quinoa, an ancient South American grain, contains lots of high-quality plant protein and is very low in gluten, so it is easily tolerated by those who are gluten sensitive. **Build your own:** Substitute other hard winter squash. You can also try bulgur, couscous, and pearl barley instead of quinoa. Leftover roasted squash can be used many ways: as a stuffing for ravioli, as an addition to vegetable soup, or stirred into lamb or beef stew. The patty mix has the texture of a potato pancake, easy to cook in a nonstick skillet but too delicate to grill.

SERVES 4

1 tablespoon honey
1 tablespoon unsalted butter, melted
Pinch of ground cinnamon
Sea salt and freshly ground black pepper
1 small butternut squash, halved and
 seeds removed
2 teaspoons plus 2 tablespoons olive oil, plus
 more as needed
$\frac{1}{2}$ cup quinoa, well rinsed
1 cup water
$\frac{1}{4}$ cup ground hazelnuts or almonds

$\frac{1}{2}$ cup potato flakes or dried bread crumbs,
 plus more as needed
1 large egg, beaten
4 slices (about 6 ounces) Gruyère cheese
4 sprouted wheat buns
4 leaves butter lettuce
1 large tomato, sliced
Caramelized Shallot Jam (page 133)
Piquillo Pepper Ketchup (page 132)
Handful baby greens
Beet Pickles (optional; page 113)

Preheat the oven to 400°F. Line a rimmed baking sheet with aluminum foil. In a small bowl, mix together the honey, butter, cinnamon, and salt and pepper to taste. Arrange the squash on the baking sheet, cut side up, allowing the rim of the sheet to support the neck of the squash to keep it level. Coat the cut sides of the squash with the butter mixture. Roast until soft throughout, about 40 minutes.

While the squash is roasting, heat 2 teaspoons of the

olive oil in a medium saucepan until hot. Add the quinoa and stir and cook until the grain is lightly toasted, about 3 minutes. Add the water and bring to a boil. Add a large pinch of salt, cover, and simmer until the grains have puffed up and are tender, about 15 minutes. Let cool, drain off any excess liquid, and fluff the grains with a fork.

Let the squash cool on the baking sheet, then scoop the squash flesh into a bowl and mash lightly. Measure 2 cups of the squash into a large bowl and reserve the remaining squash for another use. Add the quinoa to the squash with the hazelnuts, potato flakes, beaten egg, and salt and pepper to taste. Cover the bowl and refrigerate for at least 30 minutes or up to overnight.

Line a baking sheet with plastic wrap. To shape the burgers, work with damp hands. Divide and shape the patty mixture into 4 evenly sized balls. Place them on the baking sheet with plenty of space between them.

Then pat them lightly into rounds. Refrigerate the patties for at least 30 minutes before cooking.

When ready to cook, heat the remaining 2 tablespoons olive oil in a large, nonstick skillet over medium heat. Cook the burgers until nicely crusted and brown, about 3 minutes per side, turning carefully. Add more oil, if needed, to keep the burgers from sticking. For the last minute or two of cooking, drape a slice of cheese over each burger to melt.

While the burgers cook, toast the buns in a toaster oven or under the broiler, about 5 inches from the heat, until lightly toasted.

To build the burgers, arrange a lettuce leaf on each bun bottom along with a tomato slice and then a spoonful of shallot jam. Top with a burger and a spoonful of ketchup. Add a pinch of baby greens and cover with the bun tops. Serve with beet pickles on the side, if using.

LAS VEGAS VEGAN BURGER

A vegetarian burger that makes heads turn: This one, a handsome stack of grilled vegetables on a portobello mushroom bun, has proven its worth with long-lasting popularity at Burger Bar. **Build your own:** All the elements make delicious burger accompaniments, so if you have a mixed crowd of omnivores and vegetarians over for a barbecue, you can serve everyone spectacular burgers. And you might find yourself assembling more vegan burgers than you expected. You can make the Marinated Eggplant (page 108) ahead of time and have it at room temperature, or you can simply grill a fresh eggplant with the rest of the vegetables. If you want to go the extra mile, make the Grilled Onion Steaks (page 105) and add them. You can also serve the burger topped with a small pile of fried onion rings (page 106). Try a traditional basil pesto in the height of summer or omit pesto and moisten the burger with an herb-flavored olive oil.

SERVES 4

1 cup extra-virgin olive oil, plus more for brushing
1 tablespoon finely chopped fresh thyme
1 teaspoon finely chopped fresh rosemary
1 tablespoon very finely chopped garlic
Sea salt and freshly ground black pepper
8 large portobello mushrooms, $3\frac{1}{2}$ to 4 inches
    in diameter
1 pound fat zucchini (about 2 inches in diameter),
    preferably both yellow and green ones, cut
    into $\frac{1}{4}$-inch thick rounds

1 pound plum tomatoes, thickly sliced
2 large red bell peppers, cut into
    $1\frac{1}{2}$-inch-wide strips
Marinated Eggplant (page 108) or 1 large
    (about 1 pound) purple eggplant cut into
    $\frac{1}{2}$-inch-thick rounds (about 8 slices)
4 large handfuls arugula
About 2 teaspoons balsamic vinegar
    (if using fresh eggplant)
About $\frac{1}{3}$ cup Cilantro-Arugula Pesto (page 127)

Build a medium-hot fire in a barbecue. In a medium bowl, whisk together the 1 cup of olive oil, thyme, rosemary, garlic, and salt and pepper to taste.

Scrape the gills from the portobellos and arrange them on a rimmed baking sheet. Add the zucchini, tomatoes and bell peppers to the baking sheet. Brush all the vegetables with the herbed oil. If you are grilling the fresh eggplant, brush it, too, with the herbed olive oil.

Brush the grill rack with olive oil, transfer the vegetables to the grill, and cook, turning as needed and being careful not to let the olive oil flame up, until tender. The zucchini and tomatoes will be done first, needing just 2 to 3 minutes per side. The peppers will be done next. If you have been careful to just brown them, they will not need to be peeled. The mushrooms and fresh eggplant will need about 5 minutes per side.

In a medium bowl, toss the arugula with a little of the marinade from the Marinated Eggplant, if using. Otherwise, toss the arugula with some of the remaining herbed olive oil and the balsamic vinegar. Taste for seasoning and set aside.

To build the burgers, generously spread the gill side of 4 mushrooms with pesto. Top with yellow zucchini, several tomato slices, green zucchini, eggplant slices, and several strips of bell pepper. Drizzle another small spoonful of pesto over all and close with another mushroom. Arrange some of the arugula salad on the side and serve immediately.

SOUTHWESTERN BEAN BURGER

Yes, bean burgers can be moist and delicious. And they invite variation in spicing and additions. I've created a Southwest theme for these with chipotle peppers, corn, and red pepper, and then served them wrapped in flour tortillas. The patty mixture is fragile but can be shaped. And it does need to be cooked in a nonstick skillet, not grilled. **Build your own:** You might want to make more patties than you need, since they freeze well. Form the patties and wrap them individually in waxed paper or plastic wrap, then seal in a plastic bag or freezer container. Defrost them in the refrigerator before cooking. To cook your own beans, see the Feijoada Burger on page 43.

SERVES 4

About 4 tablespoons olive oil
$\frac{1}{2}$ cup finely chopped white or yellow onion
Sea salt and freshly ground black pepper
1 small red bell pepper, cut into $\frac{1}{8}$-inch dice
$\frac{1}{2}$ cup corn kernels
1 tablespoon very finely chopped chipotle
  pepper in adobo sauce
2 cups cooked black beans, very well drained
  (page 43) or one 15-ounce can black beans or
  pinto beans, rinsed and very well drained

$\frac{1}{2}$ cup dried bread crumbs
2 large eggs, beaten
1 small red onion, very thinly sliced
2 tablespoons apple cider vinegar
4 large whole-wheat tortillas
About $\frac{1}{3}$ cup Spicy Aïoli (page 125)
Grilled Avocado-Mango Salsa (page 119)

In a medium skillet, heat 2 tablespoons of the olive oil over medium-high heat until it shimmers. Add the chopped onion, a pinch of salt, and cook until the onions are soft and translucent, about 5 minutes. Add the bell pepper and corn kernels and cook until the vegetables are tender, about another 3 minutes. Stir in the chipotle and season to taste with salt and pepper.

In a large bowl, mash the beans, leaving them with a coarse texture. Add the bread crumbs, beaten eggs, and sautéed vegetables. Stir well, and taste for seasoning, adding salt and pepper to taste. Cover and refrigerate for at least 30 minutes or as long as overnight.

In a small bowl, toss the red onion with the vinegar, separating the slices into rings. Set aside.

Line a baking sheet with plastic wrap. To shape the burgers, work with damp hands. Divide and shape the patty mixture into 8 evenly sized balls. Place them on the baking sheet with plenty of space between them. Then pat them lightly into rounds. Refrigerate the patties for at least 30 minutes before cooking.

When ready to cook, heat the remaining 2 tablespoons of olive oil in a large, nonstick skillet over medium heat. Cook the burgers until nicely crusted and brown, about 2 minutes per side, turning carefully. Add more oil, if needed, to keep the burgers from sticking.

While the burgers cook, wrap the tortillas in a clean kitchen towel or napkin and microwave until warm.

To build the burgers, spread a little aïoli into the center of each tortilla. Arrange 2 burgers, slightly overlapping, on each tortilla. Spoon some salsa over them, and then top with a small tangle of the marinated red onion. Serve immediately, passing more aïoli and salsa at the table.

ON THE SIDE

PERFECT FRENCH FRIES

Perfection takes time. Three days, in fact. The long soaking leaches starch from the potatoes so they turn golden and crispy on the outside and white and fluffy on the inside. **Build your own:** Depending on how you choose to cut your potatoes, you can make fat or skinny fries, wedges or shoestrings. Skins on or off, your choice. I like to serve fries in small earthenware flowerpots. You could also fashion a cone of parchment paper and fit it inside a narrow glass as a holder, then fill the cone with fries.

SERVES 4

4 large (about 2 pounds) potatoes, preferably russets, peeled, if desired

6 to 8 cups vegetable or sunflower oil for deep frying
Coarse sea salt

Place the potatoes in a pan of cold water to cover, then let them soak overnight, refrigerated. The next day, drain and cut them. For skinny fries, cut the potatoes lengthwise into ¼-inch-thick slices. Cut these lengthwise into ¼-inch-thick strips. For fat fries, simply increase the width of your slices. For wedges, cut the potatoes lengthwise in half, then cut the halves into wedges. To make evenly sized wedges, if the potatoes are very fat, you may need to cut a lengthwise slice out of the middle of the potato and either discard it or cut it into fat fries. For shoestrings, use the julienne blade of a mandoline and cut the potatoes into very fine strips. However they are cut, place the potatoes in a bowl, cover with cold water, and again let them soak overnight, refrigerated.

When ready to fry, drain the potatoes well and pat dry with paper towels or a kitchen towel. Cover a baking sheet with several layers of paper towels. Put 2 cups of oil per potato in a deep, heavy pot or deep fryer. The oil should fill the pot at least one-third full. Heat it to 250°F. Working in batches, fry the potatoes until they are cooked through but remain almost white, about 5 minutes. Drain on the prepared baking sheet. The fries may be prepared up to this point several hours in advance. Cover and refrigerate until needed.

Just before serving, heat the oil to 360°F. Again working in batches, fry the potatoes until they are golden and crisp. The timing will depend on the size you have cut your potatoes, but allow about 3 minutes for skinny fries. When done, drain them briefly on paper towels and sprinkle liberally with salt. Scoop them into a bowl and serve immediately.

VEGETABLE CHIPS AND GAUFRETTES

A colorful pile of crisp, salty chips: what a terrific burger teammate. You can use just about any firm root vegetable, such as carrots, parsnips, beets, and potatoes, of course. Lotus root, with its lacy structure, makes particularly pretty chips. Do choose vegetables to give you a variety of colors. For long, tapered vegetables, such as carrots, look for very fat ones and use only the fattest parts. Vegetables with a high sugar content, such as beets and sweet potatoes, can burn easily, so fry at a slightly lower temperature and watch carefully. Gaufrettes are easily made if you have a mandoline with a serrated or waffle blade. They require nothing more than slicing, turning the vegetable 90 degrees between slices.

SERVES 4

6 to 8 cups vegetable or sunflower oil for deep frying
1 medium unpeeled blue potato or other potato such as Yukon gold or red bliss
About a 4-inch piece lotus root
1 medium red beet, peeled
1 fat carrot
1 fat parsnip
Coarse sea salt

Fill a deep, heavy pot or deep fryer at least one-third full of oil and heat it to 350°F. Using a mandoline, slice the vegetables paper thin.

Reserve each vegetable in a separate bowl. Potatoes should be soaked in water as soon as they are cut to prevent discoloration and to wash away some of their starch. Pat them dry with paper towels or a clean kitchen towel just before cooking. Other vegetables do not need to be soaked or rinsed.

Fry each vegetable separately in the hot oil, starting with a small test batch to make sure the oil is not too hot. You want the chips or gaufrettes to cook through and brown, not burn. Scatter them into the oil in small handfuls and turn and separate them with tongs. Fry until browned and done, about 1 minute. Using a skimmer, remove the vegetables from the oil and drain on paper towels. Season generously with salt. Scoop them into a bowl and serve immediately.

OVEN FRIES

think duck fat was created for cooking potatoes. As if fries were not addictive enough. When cooked in duck fat, well . . . prepare yourself. And, if you need an excuse for the indulgence, tell yourself you are simply using up what would otherwise be tossed out after roasting a duck or goose. If you let the fat settle and strain it, then refrigerate it in a covered container—or even freeze it—it will keep for months. **Build your own:** You can vary the flavor depending on the fat you use and the herbs you add. Red, waxy potatoes are best, as they hold their shape. You do need time to make oven fries, most of which is devoted to preheating your oven until it is really hot. But the timing is far more forgiving than for deep frying.

SERVES 4

2 pounds unpeeled red, waxy potatoes
1 head garlic, separated into cloves, unpeeled
2 to 3 tablespoons duck or goose fat, melted,
    or extra-virgin olive oil

Coarse sea salt
2 sprigs fresh rosemary

Preheat the oven to 500°F. Line a rimmed baking sheet with aluminum foil, shiny side up. This helps prevent the potatoes from sticking. Place the prepared sheet pan in the oven.

Cut the potatoes into wedges about $\frac{1}{4}$ inch thick at their widest point. In a large bowl, toss the potatoes with the garlic cloves, melted fat, plenty of salt, and the rosemary sprigs.

Carefully remove the hot pan from the oven. Quickly pour the potatoes and garlic into the pan and distribute them into an even layer. Immediately return the pan to the oven and lower the heat to 450°F. Roast until tender, about 35 minutes. You do not need to turn them during cooking.

About 5 minutes before the potatoes have finished cooking, remove the pan from the oven and loosen the potatoes. Return them to the oven to finish cooking.

Pour the potatoes and garlic into a warm serving bowl, discard the herb sprigs, season again with salt, and serve immediately.

PANISSE FRIES

In the south of France, flat breads, called *socca*, and fries, called *panisse*, made of finely ground chickpea flour make popular snacks any time of day. They have a wonderful, hearty, almost nutty flavor. The flour is easy to find in health food shops. Panisse fries are particularly good with a spicy or garlicky mayonnaise such as the Spicy Aïoli (page 125) or the Piquillo Pepper Ketchup (page 132). Make the batter a day ahead, and then the fries will cut very easily.

SERVES 6 to 8

4 cups water
Large pinch of sea salt, plus more for sprinkling
1/4 cup olive oil

2 3/4 cups (11 ounces) chickpea flour
6 to 8 cups vegetable or sunflower oil for
    deep frying

In a large saucepan, bring the water to a boil, and then lower the heat to maintain a simmer. Whisk in the salt, then the olive oil, and then slowly pour in the chickpea flour, whisking all the while.

Cook the mixture, stirring frequently and scraping all over the bottom of the pot with a wooden spoon or silicone spatula, until very thick, about 7 minutes. Immediately scrape the mixture into a food processor and process until smooth. Scrape down the work bowl several times and process again. Any lumps can cause the fries to burst when cooked.

Working very quickly to prevent a skin from forming, pour the batter into an ungreased 12 by 9 by 1/2-inch rimmed sheet pan. Make sure the pan is flat so the batter forms an even layer. Use a spatula to smooth the top. The dough will form a layer about 1/2 inch thick.

Rap the pan firmly against the counter to release any air bubbles. Lay a sheet of plastic wrap directly on the surface of the batter and gently roll a wooden dowel over the surface to work out any bubbles. Lift up the corners of the wrap to release air bubbles and smooth the wrap again. Rap the pan again against the counter to work any bubbles up to the surface and smooth again. Any bubbles may cause the fries to burst. (The fried crumbs are delicious, however.) Refrigerate for at least 2 hours and preferably overnight.

Fill a deep, heavy pot or deep fryer at least one-third full of oil and heat to 360°F. To unmold the dough, run a knife around the edges, and then turn the pan over onto a counter so 1 long side lines up with the edge of the counter. Trim the edges, if needed. To cut matchstick fries: Cut the dough crosswise into 5 strips about 2¼ inches wide. Cutting parallel to the counter, split the strips in half to create 10 strips, each 2¼ inches by ¼ inch. Cut these strips into ¼-inch-wide matchsticks. You may cut rougher, thicker fries; just cook them a minute or so longer to make sure they cook through.

Working in batches, cook the fries until they are pale gold and crisp, about 3 minutes. When done, drain them briefly on paper towels and sprinkle liberally with salt. Scoop them into a bowl and serve immediately.

ZUCCHINI FRIES

Zucchini fries can be delicious and pretty, too, with their dark green skins peeking through the golden brown, crisp coating. For more flavor, I give them a short bath in a garlicky marinade. Choose small, young zucchini. These will be meaty and nearly seedless. Use white bread crumbs so that the fries do not get too brown before the insides cook through. **Build your own:** Choose whatever herb you like best for the marinade or try a combination, like rosemary, thyme, oregano, and basil, for instance.

SERVES 4

1½ pounds small, thin zucchini
¼ cup olive oil
2 large garlic cloves, very finely chopped
2 teaspoons finely chopped fresh thyme
6 to 8 cups vegetable or sunflower oil
   for deep frying

2 cups all-purpose flour
2 cups dried white bread crumbs,
   such as panko
2 large eggs
Coarse sea salt

Cut the zucchini into 3-inch lengths and then cut these into wedges about ⅓ inch wide. Cut the wedges the same size so they will cook evenly.

In a large bowl, whisk together the olive oil, garlic, and thyme. Add the zucchini wedges and toss well. Let marinate for about 20 minutes.

Fill a deep, heavy pot at least one-third full with oil and heat to 350°F. Spread the flour and bread crumbs on separate plates (pie plates are great for this). Beat the eggs lightly in a large bowl.

Drain the fries of excess marinade and scatter them in the flour. Toss them until they are well coated, then shake off any excess flour. Dip them in the egg, then roll them in the bread crumbs until evenly coated. Fry, in small batches, until deeply browned, about 5 minutes.

Drain the fries on paper towels and season generously with salt. Scoop them into a bowl and serve immediately.

GRILLED ONION STEAKS

These are so good that you may be tempted to leave out the meat and just sandwich them into a bun with a little pesto. If you have room on the grill, double the recipe and save the extras to add to other burgers, like the Ostrich Bacon Burger (page 63) or a veggie burger.

SERVES 8

2 tablespoons olive oil, plus more for brushing

2 tablespoons Dijon mustard

2 tablespoons honey

1 tablespoon balsamic vinegar

2 large (about 10 ounces each) sweet onions, such as Vidalia or Maui

8 to 12 soaked bamboo skewers

Sea salt and freshly ground black pepper

Build a medium-hot fire in a barbecue. Clean and oil the grate.

In a small bowl, whisk together the 2 tablespoons of olive oil, mustard, honey, and vinegar. Set aside.

Peel the onions, leaving the ends intact, then cut them crosswise into $1/2$-inch-thick slices. Reserve the ends and small slices for another use. You should have about 4 good slices per onion. Holding them flat on the counter, thread one or two skewers through each slice, placing the skewers parallel and about $1\frac{1}{2}$ inches apart. Make sure one skewer goes through the centermost rings. The skewers will hold the slices together while they cook. Trim the skewers, if necessary, to fit on the grill.

When ready to cook, brush the onions on both sides with olive oil and season with salt and pepper. Arrange them on the grate and grill, turning after they have browned on the first side. Cook until they are about half done then brush them with the mustard mixture. Be careful, as the mixture may cause flare-ups. If so, move the onions to a cooler part of the grate. Turn and brush the onions with the mustard mixture several times, until tender throughout and the outsides have caramelized, about 15 minutes. Transfer the onions to a plate and keep warm. Remove the skewers before serving.

ALSACE BEER-BATTERED ONION RINGS

My grandmother in Alsace France, often fried foods in a beer batter. I remember best her fried apple slices. This kind of batter is a typical home-style dish in Alsace, where we have a long tradition of beer-making as well as fine cooking. **Build Your Own:** You can use any beer for the batter, but the amber beer adds a little sweetness that complements the onions. Cut the onions as thinly or thickly as you like.

SERVES 6

- $1\frac{1}{2}$ cups all-purpose flour plus more for dredging
- $1\frac{1}{2}$ teaspoons sugar
- 1 teaspoon paprika
- $1\frac{1}{2}$ cups (12 ounces) amber beer
- 1 teaspoon sea salt, plus more for seasoning
- $\frac{3}{4}$ teaspoon freshly ground black pepper

- 2 large eggs, separated
- 6 to 8 cups vegetable or sunflower oil for deep frying
- 3 large (8 to 10 ounces each) yellow onions, sliced about $\frac{1}{4}$ inch thick and separated into rings

In a large bowl, whisk together the flour, sugar, paprika, teaspoon of salt, and pepper, until evenly mixed. In another bowl, beat the beer with the egg yolks until well blended. Whisk the beer-egg mixture into the flour until smooth. Cover and let rest, refrigerated, for at least 1 hour or as long as overnight.

When ready to cook, fill a deep, heavy pot or deep fryer at least one-third full of oil and heat to 360°F.

Heat the oven to 200°F. In a medium bowl, beat the egg whites until they form soft peaks. Fold them into the beer batter. Dredge onions in flour and shake off excess. Dip the onion rings into the batter and then drop them, a few at a time, into the oil. Fry, turning occasionally, until golden brown and crisp, about 3 minutes. Drain on paper towels and season with salt while still hot. Keep the onions warm in a bowl in the oven until all are cooked.

MARINATED EGGPLANT

The marinade infuses the eggplant with a terrific medley of sweet, herbal flavors. Prepared this way, the eggplant retains its shape and doesn't get mushy. The marinated eggplant tastes best at room temperature or reheated in a low oven or in a dry skillet over low heat. **Build Your Own:** This makes a great addition to all kinds of sandwiches and burgers or can be served on its own, perhaps with some feta or goat cheese crumbled over it. Save the remaining marinade; it makes a delicious dressing for salads of tomato, baby spinach, or mixed greens.

SERVES 6 to 8

$2^1/_3$ cups olive oil, plus more for brushing
$^3/_4$ cup plus 3 tablespoons balsamic vinegar
6 tablespoons sherry vinegar
1 small yellow onion, thinly sliced
6 tablespoons honey
5 garlic cloves, crushed
2 bay leaves
3 sprigs fresh thyme

$1^1/_2$ teaspoons whole coriander seeds
$1^1/_2$ teaspoons sea salt
1 teaspoon freshly ground black pepper
1 large tomato, sliced
2 large (about 1 pound each) unpeeled purple eggplants, sliced crosswise into $^1/_2$-inch-thick slices

In a large saucepan, combine 2 cups of the olive oil, $^3/_4$ cup of the balsamic vinegar, 3 tablespoons of the sherry vinegar, the onion, honey, garlic, bay leaves, thyme sprigs, coriander seeds, salt, and pepper. Bring to a boil over medium-high heat, then simmer gently, uncovered, until the onion is tender and translucent, about 5 minutes. Add the tomato and return the marinade to a boil. Simmer for another 5 minutes. Keep the marinade hot until needed.

Meanwhile, brush the eggplant slices on both sides with olive oil. Heat 2 tablespoons of the olive oil in a large, nonstick skillet over medium-high heat. Cook the eggplant quickly on both sides until brown and just beginning to soften, 3 to 5 minutes. Remove the slices as they are done and arrange them in a single layer in a large, nonreactive baking dish. Add more oil to the skillet as needed. When the eggplant is cooked, remove the skillet from the heat and add the remaining 3 tablespoons of each balsamic and sherry vinegars to the skillet. Stand back so as not to get splattered. Stir and scrape all over the sides and bottom of the pan. Scrape the contents of the pan into the hot marinade.

Stir the marinade and pour it evenly all over the eggplant. Tightly cover the dish with plastic wrap and leave at room temperature overnight to marinate. The eggplant will finish "cooking" in the marinade. Refrigerate the eggplant in the marinade until needed. It is at its best within about 3 days but will keep for several days longer. To use, carefully lift each slice with a slotted spatula to allow it to drain a bit. Reheat in a low oven or in a dry pan over medium-low heat, or serve at room temperature. Strain any remaining marinade and refrigerate in a clean, covered, nonreactive container for up to a week longer to use as a salad dressing.

BRAZILIAN PICKLED VEGETABLES

Every burger needs a pickle on the plate. It's an automatic, traditional combination that just works. Pickles add texture and tang to a burger's soft, sweet meat. A small bowl of tart pickles, including carrots, onions, hot peppers, and whole garlic cloves, frequently welcomes diners to restaurant tables throughout Brazil and Mexico. Serve these with the Feijoada Burger (page 43). **Build Your Own:** You can pickle only one or several of these vegetables and leave out some of the spices, if you like.

SERVES ABOUT 16

Makes about 4 cups

2 cups white wine vinegar
1 cup water
3 tablespoons kosher salt or sea salt
1 tablespoon plus 1½ teaspoons sugar
1 tablespoon whole brown mustard seeds
2 teaspoons finely chopped fresh thyme
1 teaspoon each whole black peppercorns, pink peppercorns, coriander seeds, cumin seeds, and fennel seeds
1 teaspoon red pepper flakes, or to taste
3 whole allspice berries
2 bay leaves
2 whole star anise

2 large carrots, cut diagonally into ½-inch pieces
¼ small head cauliflower, broken into florets
1 large red bell pepper, cut into strips ⅓ inch wide
1 small bulb fennel, cut into ½-inch pieces
10 pearl onions, peeled
5 wedges fresh coconut, shelled but inner brown skin left on (optional)
2 jalapeño peppers, thinly sliced
5 whole garlic cloves, peeled
Zest of 1 orange, cut into long, thin strips
1 large handful cherry tomatoes
½ bunch fresh cilantro

To make the pickling mix: In a large, nonreactive saucepan, bring the pickling mix ingredients to a boil. Simmer, uncovered, for about 5 minutes.

Add the carrots, cauliflower, bell pepper, fennel, onions, coconut, if using, jalapeños, garlic, and orange zest. Return to a boil, and simmer for about 3 minutes. Cover, remove from the heat, and let cool to room temperature. Add the tomatoes. Pack the vegetables and brine into clean glass jars, cover, and refrigerate for at least 1 day before using. The pickles will keep for several weeks, refrigerated. To serve, scoop them into small bowls and garnish with cilantro sprigs.

BEET PICKLES

The sweet, sharp flavor of these pickles goes so well with beef burgers. Beef burgers are almost sweet and beets are sweet too, especially when baked. The pickling gives them a nice tang that refreshes the palate between bites of burger. The pickles also go particularly well with meaty, richly flavored burgers such as the Blue Cheese–Stuffed Bacon Sliders (page 15) and the Ostrich Bacon Burger (page 63). They brighten vegetarian burgers too, especially the Las Vegas Vegan Burger (page 89). **Build Your Own:** To vary the flavor of these pickles, instead of whole coriander seeds, try 1 teaspoon mustard seeds or $3/4$ teaspoon fennel seeds.

SERVES 8

Makes about 3 cups

- $2^{1}/_{2}$ pounds beets, preferably small
- $1^{1}/_{2}$ cups white distilled vinegar
- $2/_{3}$ cup water
- $1/_{2}$ cup honey
- $1/_{4}$ cup plus 1 tablespoon sugar

- $2^{1}/_{2}$ teaspoons kosher salt or sea salt
- 2 sprigs fresh thyme
- 1 teaspoon whole black peppercorns
- 1 teaspoon whole coriander seeds

Preheat the oven to 375°F. Wrap the beets tightly in aluminum foil and bake until tender, about 1 hour. The timing will depend on the size of the beets. When cool enough to handle, slip off their skins and cut the beets into wedges about $1/2$ inch thick. Put the beets in a large, nonreactive bowl and set aside.

In a large pot, bring the vinegar, water, honey, sugar, salt, thyme, peppercorns, and coriander to a boil. Simmer, uncovered, for about 5 minutes. Pour the mixture over the beets, cover tightly with plastic wrap, and leave to cool to room temperature. Refrigerate for 2 days before serving. The pickles will keep for 2 weeks. The longer they marinate, the more pronounced their flavor will be.

MARINATED FENNEL SALAD

This is a simple, crunchy, and colorful salad that works wonderfully with the Crab Sliders (page 79). **Build Your Own:** The salad also complements salmon, rock shrimp, and chicken burgers. Or serve it with a plate of roasted mussels. It can be made well ahead, even a day ahead of time. If made in advance, it "melts" a little but retains its fresh flavor and crunchy texture.

SERVES 4 to 6

1 large (about $\frac{1}{2}$ pound) bulb fennel
1 tablespoon very finely chopped fennel fronds
4 to 5 large red radishes, cut into julienne

2 tablespoons freshly squeezed lemon juice
$\frac{1}{3}$ cup extra-virgin olive oil
Sea salt and freshly ground black pepper

Trim the stalks and cut the fennel bulb in half lengthwise. Using a mandoline, cut the halves crosswise into very thin slices. Put them in a medium, nonreactive bowl and add the fennel fronds, radishes, lemon juice, and olive oil and toss well. Season to taste with salt and pepper and toss again. Cover and refrigerate for at least 3 hours and up to 1 day before serving.

CREAMY CUCUMBER SALAD

Cucumber salad makes a great addition to the Double Salmon Tartare Burgers (page 71) and the Crab Sliders (page 79). **Build Your Own:** You could serve it as well with poached sea bass or cod. When I do that, I add a tablespoon of finely chopped fresh dill to the salad. Prepare it close to serving time.

SERVES 4

1 English (hothouse) cucumber
2 tablespoons julienned red onion
$\frac{1}{4}$ cup mayonnaise

1 tablespoon plus $1\frac{1}{2}$ teaspoons heavy cream
1 tablespoon Dijon mustard
Sea salt and freshly ground black pepper

Peel the cucumber lengthwise in alternating strips of green and white. Cut it in half lengthwise and scoop out the seeds with a spoon. Cut the halves crosswise into very thin slices and place in a bowl with the red onion. In a small bowl, whisk together the mayonnaise, cream, mustard, and salt and pepper to taste. Fold the mayonnaise mixture into the cucumbers a spoonful at a time. You want the cucumbers to be just lightly dressed.

MARINATED VEGETABLE SALAD

This salad provides a tart and crunchy accompaniment for beef, poultry, or seafood burgers. Try it with the Ostrich Bacon Burger (page 63) or the Black and Blue Burger (page 31). I've given the recipe a Spanish twist by using nut oil and sherry vinegar, and smoked paprika. **Build your own:** You can substitute any firm, crunchy vegetable in season, such as zucchini, pattypan squash, or fennel. Cut all the vegetables into an evenly sized small dice. You can replace the nut oil with another or extra-virgin olive oil and the sherry vinegar with red wine vinegar. If you like more spice, add some minced fresh hot pepper or a bit more of the hot paprika.

SERVES 4

3 tablespoons toasted hazelnut oil
1 tablespoon sherry vinegar
$\frac{1}{4}$ teaspoon smoked hot paprika, or to taste
$\frac{1}{2}$ cup carrot cut into $\frac{1}{4}$-inch dice
$\frac{1}{2}$ cup celery cut into $\frac{1}{4}$-inch dice

$\frac{1}{2}$ cup red bell pepper cut into $\frac{1}{4}$-inch dice
$\frac{1}{2}$ cup red onion cut into $\frac{1}{4}$-inch dice
$1\frac{1}{2}$ tablespoons finely chopped fresh chives
$1\frac{1}{2}$ tablespoons finely chopped fresh cilantro
Sea salt and freshly ground black pepper

In a medium, nonreactive, whisk together the oil, vinegar, and paprika. Add the carrot, celery, bell pepper, onion, chives and cilantro and toss together well. Taste and adjust seasoning with salt and pepper. Toss again, cover, and leave to marinate for at least 30 minutes before serving, or refrigerate for up to 1 day. Let come to room temperature before serving.

HEIRLOOM CHERRY TOMATO SALAD

This quick, colorful salad tastes great as a burger relish or accompaniment. For the best flavor, use local, sweet, ripe, organic cherry tomatoes. And choose a medley of colors and shapes. **Build your own:** The combination also makes a great pasta sauce—just toss it with hot pasta and add a splash of extra-virgin olive oil for aroma. For a summer party, make the salad and use it as a topping for grilled bread. You will not believe how good it tastes. As the salad sits, the tomatoes will release some of their juices. When using the salad to serve with burgers, use the juices to moisten the bun bottoms.

SERVES 4

1 tablespoon extra-virgin olive oil
$1\frac{1}{2}$ teaspoons sherry vinegar or cider vinegar
1 teaspoon finely chopped fresh tarragon or basil
1 garlic clove, very finely chopped

Pinch of freshly grated lemon zest
1 pint box heirloom cherry tomatoes in various colors, halved
Sea salt and freshly ground black pepper

In a medium, nonreactive bowl, whisk together the olive oil, vinegar, tarragon, garlic, and lemon zest. Add the tomatoes and toss well. Taste and adjust the seasoning with salt and pepper. Let sit at room temperature for about 30 minutes to let the flavors develop. The salad can be made up to 3 hours ahead; do not refrigerate.

GRILLED AVOCADO–MANGO SALSA

This salsa adds a colorful, crunchy accent to the Brazilian Rock Shrimp Burger (page 77) and would taste equally fine with roasted chicken or pork, or even with fish or shrimp tacos. **Build your own:** Serve the salsa in a grilled avocado half. Grilling the avocado adds a smoky component to the salsa but is a step that can easily be skipped. You could add papaya or substitute it for the mango, use basil or parsley instead of cilantro, lemon instead of lime, and a seeded, diced hot pepper. If you love fresh coconut, small pieces would make a great addition, too.

SERVES 4 TO 6

Makes about 1½ cups

1 ripe but firm avocado, peeled, pitted

2 tablespoons extra-virgin olive oil plus more for brushing

½ ripe mango, peeled, pitted, cut into ¼-inch dice

3 tablespoons diced red onion

2 tablespoons (or more) freshly squeezed lime juice

2 tablespoons peeled jicama or water chestnuts (fresh or canned) cut into ¼-inch dice

2 tablespoons red bell pepper cut into ¼-inch dice

1 tablespoon chopped fresh cilantro

1 small garlic clove, very finely chopped

Sea salt and freshly ground black pepper

Cut the avocado into ¼-inch-thick slices. Heat a grill pan over medium-high heat until hot or build a medium fire in a barbecue. Brush the avocado slices and the grill pan or grill rack with oil. Grill the slices quickly, about 1 minute per side, until just lightly charred. Cut into ¼-inch dice.

In a medium bowl, fold together the avocado, mango, red onion, 2 tablesppons of lime juice, jicama, bell pepper, cilantro, garlic, and the 2 tablespoons of olive oil. Mix gently until well blended and adjust the seasoning as needed with salt, pepper, and lime juice. Cover and refrigerate until needed. The salsa can be made up to 2 hours ahead and refrigerated, covered. Serve cold.

FRUIT FRIES

Colorful and playful, this light and flavorful fruit compote makes a wonderful side dish for Breakfast Burgers (page 51). The cracked black pepper cuts the sweetness and gives a little crunch, too. **Build your own:** Farmers are growing many more types of melons today and they would all work in this recipe, even seedless watermelon. If it is firm, it won't break apart when cut and tossed with the other ingredients. You can also serve the dish as a light dessert teamed with shortbread cookies.

SERVES 4

½ small, ripe honeydew melon seeded
½ small, ripe cantaloupe seeded
½ cup dessert wine, such as a
    late-harvest Riesling

2 tablespoons julienned fresh mint
Cracked black pepper

Cut the melons into thick matchsticks ¼ or ⅓ inch thick and 2 inches long. Place in a bowl and toss gently with the wine, mint, and cracked pepper to taste. Cover and refrigerate for at least 30 minutes and up to several hours. Serve cold.

ENDIVE-APPLE SALAD

This easy, quick salad adds cool crunch and a touch of sweet moistness to Mustard Seed Chicken Burgers (page 55). **Build your own:** It would work just as well with seafood or vegetarian burgers. For extra color, use one head each of white and red endive, if you happen to find the latter in your market. To keep the flavor fresh, make the salad close to serving time.

SERVES 4

2 tablespoons pine nuts
2 tablespoons extra-virgin olive oil
2 teaspoons sherry vinegar
Sea salt and freshly ground black pepper

2 small heads endive
1 small, tart green apple
1 tablespoon finely chopped fresh chives

In a small, dry pan, toast the pine nuts over medium heat until lightly browned, about 3 minutes. Be careful not to overcook; pine nuts burn easily. Immediately pour the nuts onto a saucer to cool.

In a medium bowl, whisk together the olive oil, vinegar, and salt and pepper to taste. Cut the endive crosswise into thin slices and toss them with the dressing. Quarter and core the apple. Slice the quarters thinly crosswise, and then cut the slices into matchsticks. Toss these with the endive. Add the pine nuts and chives, toss well, and taste for seasoning. Toss again just before serving.

SAUCE
IT UP

SAUCE IT UP

SPICY AÏOLI

If you like rich spiciness, you will love this sauce. Slather it on any burger and use it as a dip for all kinds of fries. The heat releases the heady aromas of garlic and spice. Fresh chile powder has the best flavor. You can make your own by grinding whole dried chipotles in a spice or coffee mill. **Build your own:** If you want even more heat, fold in only a few drops of hot sauce, because sometimes, adding too much chile powder can result in a bitter flavor.

MAKES ABOUT 1¼ CUPS

2 garlic cloves
2 large egg yolks
1 tablespoon Dijon mustard
1 tablespoon freshly squeezed orange juice
$1/_3$ teaspoon chipotle chile powder, or more to taste

Sea salt and freshly ground black pepper
1 cup olive oil
1 tablespoon plus $1/_2$ teaspoons roughly chopped fresh cilantro
1 teaspoon freshly grated orange zest

In a food processor, finely chop the garlic. Add the egg yolks, mustard, orange juice, chile powder, and a good pinch of salt. Process until well blended. With the machine running, begin adding the oil, at first drop by drop, and then increasing to a slow stream as the mixture forms an emulsion. Pulse in the cilantro and zest. Transfer the mayonnaise to a container and season to taste with salt and pepper. Cover and refrigerate until needed, or for up to 4 days.

GREEN PEPPERCORN AND LEMON MAYONNAISE

This mayonnaise has a fresh and snappy flavor that perks up seafood and meat alike. **Build your own:** Food processors make the method nearly foolproof. However, if you are short on time, you can always jazz up store-bought mayonnaise with the flavorings.

MAKES ABOUT 1¼ CUPS

2 teaspoons brined green peppercorns
2 large egg yolks
1 tablespoon Dijon mustard
1 tablespoon freshly squeezed lemon juice

Sea salt and freshly ground black pepper
1 cup olive oil
2 teaspoons freshly grated lemon zest

Rinse and drain the peppercorns, and then crush them slightly with the side of a knife. Set aside.

Put the egg yolks, mustard, lemon juice, and a pinch of salt in a food processor and process until well blended. With the machine running, begin adding the oil, at first drop by drop, and then increasing to a slow stream as the mixture forms an emulsion. Pulse in the lemon zest, reserved peppercorns, and salt and pepper to taste. Transfer the mayonnaise to a container, cover, and refrigerate until needed, or for up to 4 days.

CILANTRO-ARUGULA PESTO

The color of this pesto is as vibrant as its flavor. The combination of cilantro, lime, and macadamia nuts gives this pesto a South American twist. It's a welcome addition to just about any burger you can think of.

MAKES ABOUT 1¼ CUPS

1 large bunch fresh cilantro
12 roasted, salted macadamia nuts
1 or 2 garlic cloves, to your taste
2 cups packed arugula
1 teaspoon freshly squeezed lime juice

$\frac{1}{3}$ teaspoon freshly grated lime zest
6 tablespoons extra-virgin olive oil
$\frac{1}{4}$ cup freshly grated Pecorino Romano cheese
Sea salt and freshly ground black pepper

Trim the larger stems off the cilantro and discard them. Put the nuts and garlic in a food processor and process until they are finely chopped. Add the cilantro, arugula, lime juice, and lime zest, and process until you have a coarse purée. With the machine running, add the olive oil in a thin stream and process until smooth. Scrape down the sides as necessary. Pulse in the cheese and season to taste with salt and pepper. Transfer the pesto to a container, cover, and refrigerate until needed, or for up to 2 days.

TAPENADE

apenade, an intensely flavored purée of black olives, anchovies, and seasonings, has a natural affinity for meat, especially beef and lamb. It adds deep, rich, slightly pungent flavors. **Build your own:** In the south of France in summertime, tapenade is smeared on crusty bread and served with plates of charcuterie meats and pâté. Try the tapenade with lamb burgers and buffalo burgers. Leftovers are wonderful to have on hand for a quick snack or as a sandwich with goat cheese.

MAKES ABOUT 1½ CUPS

1⅓ cups pitted brine-cured black olives,
   such as kalamata
4 oil-packed anchovy fillets, drained (optional)
2 tablespoons capers, drained
2 tablespoons olive oil
3 large garlic cloves, peeled
Leaves from 10 sprigs fresh flat-leaf parsley or
   basil or a mix of both

Leaves from 2 or 3 sprigs fresh thyme
2 teaspoons cognac or brandy
1 teaspoon Dijon mustard
1 teaspoon freshly squeezed lemon juice
Pinch of freshly ground black pepper

Put the olives, anchovies, capers, olive oil, garlic, parsley, thyme, cognac, mustard, lemon juice, and pepper in a food processor or blender. Process, stopping to scrape the sides occasionally, until you have a fairly smooth purée. No salt is needed because the anchovies and olives are fairly salty. Transfer the tapenade to a container and set aside until needed. The tapenade keeps, covered and refrigerated, for up to a week.

OLD-FASHIONED MUSTARD

At our restaurants, we use a strong mustard I have not seen on supermarket or specialty store shelves. But, by simply adding soaked mustard seeds to commercially prepared Dijon mustard, the flavor becomes intense and satisfying. And the seeds pop against your teeth with a little explosion of spice. **Build your own:** Use the mustard as you normally would—in vinaigrettes, mayonnaise, cream sauces, and, of course, with your burgers. A small, decorative jar of the mustard would make a welcomed hostess gift. On their own, the soaked mustard seeds make a fun garnish for many dishes.

MAKES ABOUT 1¾ CUPS

$1/4$ cup whole yellow mustard seeds
2 tablespoons whole brown mustard seeds
$3/4$ cup dry white wine

2 tablespoons white wine vinegar
Pinch of sea salt
$1^1/4$ cups Dijon mustard

Combine the yellow and brown mustard seeds in a medium saucepan with the white wine, vinegar, and salt. Bring to a boil over medium-high heat, and immediately pour the mixture into a medium bowl. Cover and set aside at room temperature overnight.

Drain the seeds through a fine-mesh sieve. Discard the liquid. In a medium bowl, fold the seeds into the Dijon mustard until evenly mixed. Transfer the mustard to 1 or 2 small containers, cover, and refrigerate for 1 to 2 days to let the flavors develop. The mustard keeps, refrigerated, for up to a month.

SPICY RED PEPPER-TOMATO RELISH

This versatile relish has a wonderful, summery taste. Serve it warm or at room temperature. Since it is basically a combination of tomatoes and onions, it tastes great with just about any burger. **Build your own:** Any extras make a great accompaniment to roast lamb, fish, chicken, or polenta. For a more elegant preparation, purée the relish in a blender and then strain it to make a smooth, unctuous sauce.

1 large red bell pepper
2 tablespoons olive oil, plus more for brushing
6 fresh basil leaves
1 large yellow onion, finely chopped
¾ pound (about 5 medium) plum tomatoes, peeled, seeded, and chopped

1 to 2 jalapeño peppers, to your taste, seeds removed and finely chopped
2 garlic cloves, very finely chopped
1 teaspoon finely chopped fresh thyme
1 teaspoon sugar or honey, or to taste
Sea salt and freshly ground black pepper

Preheat the broiler and adjust the rack to about 5 inches below the flame. Brush the pepper all over with olive oil and broil it, turning frequently, until it is blackened on all sides. (You can also roast the pepper over the open flame of a gas burner or on an outdoor grill.) Remove the pepper to a bowl, cover, and let rest until cool enough to handle. Pull off the charred skin and remove the stem and seeds. Cut the pepper into ¼-inch dice and set aside.

Stack the basil leaves and fold them in half along their spines. Cut them crosswise into very fine strips and set aside.

In a saucepan over medium heat, warm 1 tablespoon of the olive oil. Add the onion and cook until soft and translucent, about 5 minutes. Add the roasted pepper, tomatoes, jalapeño, garlic, thyme, sugar, and salt and pepper to taste. Bring to a simmer and cook until the tomatoes soften and the flavors meld, about 5 minutes. Do not overcook; the tomatoes should retain their shape. Stir in the basil and taste for seasoning. Adjust with more salt, pepper, and sugar, if needed. The relish should be chunky and moist but not saucy.

Transfer the relish to a container and stir in the remaining 1 tablespoon of olive oil. Cover and set aside at room temperature until needed. The relish keeps, refrigerated, for up to 3 days. Bring to room temperature or reheat gently over low heat before serving.

PIQUILLO PEPPER KETCHUP

Roasted peppers and tomatoes make an unbeatable combination. Piquillo peppers, with their smoky, sweet piquancy, have a unique and irresistible flavor. Piquillos, a trademark ingredient of Spanish cooking, are a variety of sweet red pepper that is roasted over oak fires and hand peeled. They can be found, jarred, in specialty food shops. Keeping a jar of these delicious peppers on your pantry shelf is a good habit to fall into. **Build your own:** You can substitute roasted sweet bell peppers, but the ketchup will not have quite the same wonderful, aromatic flavor.

MAKES ABOUT 2 CUPS

2 tablespoons olive oil
$\frac{1}{2}$ cup finely chopped yellow onion
1 pound (about 7 medium) plum tomatoes, peeled, seeded, and chopped
One 12-ounce jar piquillo peppers, roughly chopped (about 1 cup)

$\frac{1}{4}$ cup white wine vinegar, plus more to taste
2 teaspoons honey or sugar, plus more to taste
2 garlic cloves, very finely chopped
1 teaspoon finely chopped fresh thyme
Sea salt and freshly ground black pepper

In a saucepan, heat 1 tablespoon of the olive oil over medium heat. Add the onion and cook until soft and translucent, about 5 minutes. Add the tomatoes, peppers, $\frac{1}{4}$ cup of vinegar, 2 teaspoons of honey, garlic, thyme, and salt and pepper to taste. Bring to a simmer and cook, uncovered, until the mixture is very thick, about 15 minutes, stirring frequently so the ketchup does not scorch.

Transfer the mixture to a blender or food processor and purée until smooth. Taste for seasoning and adjust with salt, pepper, honey, and vinegar as needed. The ketchup should have a good balance of sweet and tart. Pour the ketchup into a container and stir in the remaining 1 tablespoon olive oil. Cover and set aside at room temperature until needed. The ketchup keeps, refrigerated, for up to a week. It may also be frozen for up to 4 months.

CARAMELIZED SHALLOT JAM

This jam has an intense, sweet-tart, almost raisin-like character. As the shallots slowly cook, they melt into a savory, sweet, jam-like mass. A small spoonful tastes great alongside burgers as well as roast pork or chicken. **Build your own:** When figs are in season, chop a few and add them to the shallots while they cook. Or, soak dried figs until soft, drain, chop, and add. The recipe can easily be doubled or even tripled.

MAKES ABOUT 1 CUP

2 tablespoons olive oil
2 cups finely chopped shallots
Sea salt
$1\frac{1}{2}$ teaspoons finely chopped fresh thyme

$\frac{1}{4}$ cup sugar
About 1 tablespoon water
2 tablespoons aged balsamic vinegar
Freshly ground black pepper

In a large skillet, heat the oil over medium heat until hot. Add the shallots, stir, and season with a pinch of salt. Cook, stirring occasionally, for 5 minutes, then add the thyme. Continue to cook, stirring occasionally, until the shallots are light gold and have thoroughly melted, about 15 more minutes. Stir more often toward the end of cooking to make sure the shallots do not stick and burn.

While the shallots are cooking, in a small saucepan, heat the sugar with the water over medium-high heat, stirring until the sugar is dissolved. Cook at a boil, un-covered and without stirring, until the sugar caramelizes to a medium amber color, about 5 minutes. Remove the pan from the heat and add the vinegar. The mixture will foam and spit, so stand back to avoid being splattered. Return the pan to low heat, and stir until the caramel has melted.

Scrape the shallots into the caramel and stir well. Transfer the mixture to a container, cover, and set aside to cool. Taste for seasoning, and adjust with salt and pepper. The jam keeps, refrigerated, for up to a week. It may also be frozen for up to 4 months. Bring to room temperature before using.

GRENADINE PICKLED ONIONS

The onions emerge from their pickling bath a Christmas red color. Their refreshing balance of sweet-tartness makes a welcome addition to richly flavored dishes such as beef burgers, as well as duck and game dishes.

MAKES ABOUT 2 CUPS

1 teaspoon whole black peppercorns
$^{1}/_{2}$ teaspoon whole coriander seeds
1 cup red wine vinegar

$^{1}/_{2}$ cup grenadine
1 large (about 10 ounces) red onion,
   thinly sliced

Tie the peppercorns and coriander seeds in cheesecloth or put them in a tea ball. In a nonreactive saucepan over medium-high heat, bring the vinegar, grenadine, and spices to a boil. Add the onion and simmer, uncovered, for 10 to 15 minutes. Let cool, transfer to a nonreactive container, cover, and let sit for 2 hours before using. The onion will turn a deeper color and take on more flavor if left in the pickling mixture for a day or two before use. They keep, refrigerated, for up to 2 weeks.

SHALLOT-TARRAGON BUTTER

This delicious, make-ahead flavored (compound) butter is a pretty yellow color dotted with red from the wine-cooked shallots and green from the tarragon. I've never understood why compound butters fell out of fashion. With the increasing popularity of burger and steak restaurants, these tasty and practical concoctions are making a comeback. **Build your own:** This compound butter can be flavored with different herbs, citrus juice and zest, even hot pepper if you like. As the pat of butter melts on the hot burger, it releases its aromas, creating a heady experience.

ABOUT 10 SERVINGS

MAKES About 1/2 pound

2 sticks ($^{1}/_{2}$ pound) unsalted butter, softened, plus 2 teaspoons for cooking

2 teaspoons olive oil

$^{1}/_{4}$ cup very finely chopped shallot

$^{1}/_{3}$ cup dry red wine

1 tablespoon finely chopped fresh tarragon

Sea salt and freshly ground black pepper

In a small saucepan, heat 2 teaspoons of butter and the olive oil over medium heat until hot. Add the shallot, and cook without browning, stirring occasionally, until the shallot is tender and translucent, about 5 minutes. Add the wine, bring to a boil, and cook until the pan is nearly dry. Stir in the tarragon and season to taste with salt and pepper. Let cool.

In a medium bowl, mash together the shallot mixture with the 2 sticks of softened butter. The butter can be used immediately, or lay a sheet of plastic wrap on the counter and scrape the butter mixture onto it. Shape the butter into a log, $1^{1}/_{2}$ inches in diameter, and enclose it in the wrap. The butter keeps for about 1 week, refrigerated, or in the freezer for up to 3 months. Cut a $^{1}/_{3}$-inch-thick slice per serving.

RED WINE, THYME, AND SHALLOT SAUCE

This is a classic French sauce we make at my restaurant Fleur de Lys to serve with all kinds of meat or even roasted chicken. I had an idea it might be a great sauce for burgers—and for dipping french fries. Cornstarch is used frequently to thicken clear—not creamy—sauces. When it is first added, the sauce may look cloudy. But after cooking for 6 or 7 minutes, the sauce will clear and take on a lovely sheen.

MAKES ABOUT 1 CUP

2 teaspoons olive oil
2 tablespoons very finely chopped shallot
1 garlic clove, very finely chopped
$1/_2$ cup dry red wine
$1^1/_2$ cups Quick Chicken Stock (page 7) or packaged low-sodium chicken broth
$1^1/_2$ teaspoons finely chopped fresh thyme
1 tablespoon ruby port
$1^1/_2$ teaspoons cornstarch
Sea salt and freshly ground black pepper
1 tablespoon unsalted butter

In a medium saucepan, heat the olive oil over medium heat. Add the shallot and cook, without browning, stirring occasionally, until the shallot is tender and translucent, about 5 minutes. Add the garlic, stir, and cook for another minute. Add the wine, bring to a boil, and cook until the pan is nearly dry, about 5 minutes. Swirl the pan as the wine reduces in order to see clearly to the bottom of the pan. Stir in the stock and thyme and return the sauce to a gentle simmer.

In a small bowl, stir together the port and cornstarch. Whisk this mixture into the sauce and continue to simmer gently, uncovered, for 6 to 10 minutes. Taste for seasoning and adjust with salt and pepper. The sauce can be made a day ahead and refrigerated, covered. Reheat gently over low heat. Just before serving, swirl in the butter.

FRIED HERBS

Fried herbs taste delicious, look beautiful, and are a snap to prepare ahead of time. **Build your own:** Use this technique for parsley, young celery leaves, sage, basil, or whatever small, tender leaf catches your imagination. You can also fry thinly sliced garlic and thinly sliced peeled ginger. The ginger makes a fun—and spicy—garnish for burgers such as the Brazilian Rock Shrimp Burger (page 77).

MAKES ABOUT 1½ CUPS

1 bunch fresh herbs such as flat-leaf parsley, basil, and sage

2 cups vegetable or sunflower oil for deep frying

Pick over the herbs, reserving the leaves and discarding the stems. Pat the leaves dry with paper towels. Heat the oil in a deep saucepan over medium-high heat to 350°F. Have a splatter guard ready. Toss the herbs into the oil and immediately place the guard over the pot. When the hissing and spitting stops after a few seconds (timing will depend on how tender the leaves are; sage will take longer and basil less time), skim out the fried herbs and drain on paper towels. Store in a covered container at room temperature until needed. The fried herbs can be made a day or two ahead.

GRAND
FINALES

CHOCOLATE-HAZELNUT BURGER

You might call it a *trompe l'oeil* burger, but there is nothing tricky about its flavors. Rich chocolate ganache forms the burger. A mango gelée masquerades as American cheese. Under the sweet bun, you will discover whipped cream "mayonnaise," fresh mint "lettuce," kiwi "pickles," and strawberry sauce "ketchup." **Build your own:** The recipe may look labor-intensive, but all the pieces can be completed well ahead and then assembled at serving time. The chocolate burger recipe may be doubled and keeps, covered and refrigerated, for 1 week. You can also shape the mixture with a melon baller into small, round truffles and roll them in cocoa powder, ground nuts, or shredded coconut.

SERVES 4

Mango Gelée

1 cup unsweetened mango purée
2 to 6 tablespoons sugar, to taste

2 tablespoons (two $1/4$-ounce packages) unflavored powdered gelatin
$1/2$ cup heavy cream

Chocolate-Hazelnut Burgers

16 to 20 whole hazelnuts
$1/2$ cup heavy cream
4 ounces bittersweet chocolate (at least 60% cacao), broken into small pieces

1 tablespoon unsalted butter, softened
1 teaspoon hazelnut liqueur or amaretto (optional)

1 pint basket ripe strawberries
1 tablespoon plus 1 teaspoon sugar plus more if needed
$1/2$ cup heavy cream

4 glazed doughnuts without central holes or filling or other sweet bun such as brioche
1 large kiwi, peeled and very thinly sliced
12 fresh mint leaves (optional)

To make the gelée:

In a small, nonreactive saucepan, stir together the mango purée and sugar, adding the sugar by tablespoonfuls until the sweet-tart balance reaches your preference. Whisk in the gelatin until well mixed and set aside to soften for 2 minutes.

Prepare an ice-water bath by emptying a tray of ice cubes into a pan of cold water. Line a 12 by 9-inch baking pan or baking sheet with plastic wrap. Place the saucepan with the mango mixture over low heat, add the cream, and cook, while whisking gently to prevent sticking and scorching, until the mixture comes to a boil, about 4 minutes. Move the saucepan off the heat and into the ice-water bath. Whisk until the mixture has cooled to room temperature. Skim off any foam with a shallow spoon.

Pour the gelée into the prepared pan. Refrigerate until set, about 1 hour. It keeps, covered and refrigerated, for 4 days.

To make the burgers:

In a small, dry skillet, toast the nuts over medium heat, tossing frequently, until evenly light brown, about 5 minutes. Wrap the hot nuts in a clean kitchen towel and rub them against each other to rid them of their papery skins. Cut the nuts in half and reserve.

In a small saucepan over medium heat, bring the cream to a boil. Put the chocolate in a medium bowl and pour the hot cream over the chocolate. Cover, and let sit for 5 minutes. Then whisk until the chocolate is melted and smooth. Whisk in the butter and liqueur, if using. Let cool, stir in the hazelnuts, cover, and then refrigerate until stiff, about 1 hour.

Line a 3-inch round cookie cutter (or whatever size fits your bun) with a sheet of plastic wrap. Leave sev-eral inches of wrap hanging over the edge. Scoop one-quarter of the chocolate mixture into the mold. Use the wrap to smooth the ganache into a disc about $1/2$ inch high. Gently lift out the burger in its wrap and refrigerate until needed. Repeat to shape the remaining 3 burgers.

Preheat the oven to 350°F. Choose 4 of the largest strawberries and cut them into very thin length-wise slices. Purée the remaining berries in a food processor with about 1 tablespoon sugar (more or less to taste).

In a small bowl, beat the cream with the remaining 1 teaspoon sugar (more or less to taste) until it forms soft mounds.

Cut the buns in half horizontally and place on a bak-ing sheet, cut side down. Warm them in the oven for about 2 minutes. They should not be too hot or they will melt the chocolate burgers.

Use the plastic wrap to transfer the mango gelée onto a work surface. With a small, sharp knife, cut the gelée into 3-inch squares, cutting through the plastic wrap as well.

To build the burgers, place each bun bottom on a dessert plate. Top each with a dollop of whipped cream, a circle of overlapping kiwi slices, and then berry slices, points outward. Add the chocolate burgers.

With the tip of a small knife, pry up a corner of each square of gelée from its plastic wrap and peel it off. Arrange the gelée on the burgers. Cover with the bun tops and tuck a few fresh mint leaves under the top buns, if using. If necessary, secure the top buns with toothpicks. Spoon a little strawberry sauce around the burgers and serve immediately.

S'MORE BURGER

S'mores may not have been part of my childhood, but they certainly were for many of my American friends. And so it made sense to create a S'more burger. Sarah Kosikowski helped create this very easy recipe. The marshmallow started as a home recipe. All the elements for this dessert can be completed ahead of time and then warmed for assembly. Several steps in the recipe are easiest and most quickly done if you have a small propane torch. Propane pastry torches can now be found in kitchenware shops, but I think the least expensive and best option is to buy one from the hardware store. It delivers more power and control. And you will find all sorts of culinary uses for it once you get comfortable with it. **Build your own:** You could simplify the presentation by just making 8 single burgers sandwiched between 2 larger pastry squares or rounds.

SERVES 8

One $1/2$-pound frozen puff pastry sheet

$1/2$ cup sugar

Chocolate Sauce

$3/4$ cup heavy cream
$1/2$ cup sugar
$1/2$ cup water

8 ounces bittersweet chocolate (60% cacao), broken into pieces

Marshmallow Burgers

1 cup light corn syrup
$3/4$ cup sugar
$1/4$ cup water
3 large egg whites

1 tablespoon vanilla extract
Sliced fruit such as fresh figs (optional)
Fresh mint leaves (optional)

Preheat the oven to 400°F. Set the pastry sheet on a work counter and let it defrost just until it can be worked, about 10 minutes. Unfold the pastry, if necessary, then lightly dust the counter and pastry with flour and roll the sheet out into an 16 by 12-inch rectangle. Prick it well all over and sprinkle the sugar evenly over the pastry. Cut the pastry lengthwise into 6 even strips about 2 inches wide. Cut each of these crosswise into 4 even pieces. You should have 24 pieces, each about 4 inches by 2 inches.

Line a baking sheet with a nonstick baking mat or parchment paper. Very carefully transfer the pastry pieces to the prepared sheet. Cover with another nonstick baking mat or parchment and weight the pastry down by sitting another baking sheet on top. Bake about 10 minutes, remove the top sheet, and bake until the pastry is golden, shiny, and very crisp, about 5 minutes more. Rotate the pan halfway through baking.

The sugar may be unevenly melted. If you have a propane torch, carefully caramelize the sugar on the pastry to give the squares a dark brown, very shiny coating. (These are also good to eat on their own.) Set aside until needed. The pastry can be completed up to this point several hours ahead of time.

To make the chocolate sauce:
In a medium saucepan over medium heat, bring the cream, sugar, and water, to a full boil, stirring just until the sugar dissolves. Put the chocolate in a medium bowl and pour the hot cream mixture over it. Cover and let sit for 5 minutes. Whisk until smooth. Set aside, and keep warm until needed. The sauce can be made ahead of time and reheated on low in a microwave oven. This makes about 2 cups of a beautifully glossy, pourable sauce.

To make the marshmallow
burgers: In a medium saucepan over medium-high heat, bring the sugar, corn syrup, and water to a boil, stirring just until the sugar dissolves. Using a candy thermometer, continue to cook the syrup, without stirring, until it reaches 250°F.

Meanwhile, when the sugar syrup reaches about 225°F, in the bowl of a stand mixer fitted with the whisk attachment, beat the egg whites on high until they form soft, glossy peaks. When the sugar reaches 250°F, with the mixer beating on high, very slowly add the sugar syrup to the whites.

Continue to beat until the mixture is very stiff and just slightly warm, about 10 minutes. As the mixture stiffens, you may have to slow the mixer a bit so it does not overheat. Beat in the vanilla. Immediately scrape the mixture into a pastry bag fitted with a fat, round tip.

To build the burgers, pipe a marshmallow patty on 16 of the pastry pieces. Brown the marshmallow with a propane torch. Stack 8 of the assembled burgers on the other 8 and close the burgers with the remaining 8 pastry pieces. Arrange a sliced fig, if using, on the top, and add a final small dollop of marshmallow. The burgers can be prepared to this point several hours ahead of time, if desired, and left at room temperature.

When ready to serve, arrange the burgers on dessert plates, garnish with a few mint leaves, if using, and drizzle the warm chocolate sauce over and around them. Serve immediately.

CREAMY CHEESECAKE BURGER

Laurent Pillard, chef of Burger Bar and Sleek Steakhouse/Ultra-Lounge, created this dessert burger. Caramelized pineapple makes a great flavor combination with the creamy cheesecake. The simple cheesecake mix stays soft even after baking. This makes it possible to shape it into burgers with no fuss at all. And it can be made ahead of time, leaving just the assembly to complete before serving. **Build your own:** You can leave out the pineapple and replace the raspberries with other berries.

SERVES 8

Cheesecake

$^1/_2$ cup half-and-half
$^1/_2$ cup heavy cream
$^1/_2$ cup sugar

1 large pineapple, peeled, cored, and cut
    into 8 rounds
3 tablespoons unsalted butter
$^1/_4$ cup sugar
8 glazed doughnuts without holes or filling or 1
    large loaf brioche or challah, sliced

1 vanilla bean or 1 tablespoon vanilla extract
12 ounces cream cheese, at room temperature
2 large eggs

1 pint basket raspberries
1 tablespoon plus 2 teaspoons sugar,
    plus more if needed
1 cup heavy cream
8 small fresh mint sprigs

To make the cheesecake:

Combine the half-and-half, cream, and sugar in a medium saucepan. Split the vanilla bean lengthwise, if using, and scrape the seeds into the cream. Bring the cream to a boil over medium heat, stirring well to make sure the sugar is dissolved.

In the bowl of a stand mixer, whisk the cream cheese until smooth. Add the eggs, one at a time, beating until well incorporated and smooth. With the machine on low, slowly whisk the hot cream mixture into the cream cheese. Add the vanilla extract now, if using. Whisk until smooth. Pour the mixture through a fine-mesh strainer into an 8-inch square baking pan, cover with aluminum foil, and refrigerate for 30 minutes.

Preheat the oven to 350°F. Bring a kettle of water to a boil.

Place the cheesecake mix, covered, in a larger, deep pan and put in the oven. Carefully pour the boiling water into the larger pan until the level reaches halfway up the sides of the cheesecake pan. Bake until the center of the cheesecake mixture just wobbles slightly and the edges are set, 30 to 45 minutes. Refrigerate until cold. Whisk the cheesecake mix until smooth and scrape it into a pastry bag fitted with a fat round or star tip. Or simply re-cover the whisked mixture and refrigerate until needed. It keeps for up to 3 days.

Preheat the oven to 350°F. Keeping in mind that the pineapple slices will shrink slightly as they cook, trim them to fit your buns, if necessary. To cook the pineapple, melt the butter in a large skillet over medium to medium-low heat. Stir in the sugar. Then add the pineapple slices to the skillet and cook until lightly golden on both sides, about 10 minutes. Be very careful toward the end of cooking, as the cooking liquids will caramelize and can burn quickly if you are not watching. Keep warm but not hot.

Cut the buns in half horizontally and place them on a baking sheet, cut side down. Warm them in the oven for about 2 minutes. They should not be too hot or they will melt the burgers. Purée the raspberries with 1 tablespoon sugar. Taste and add more sugar, if needed. In a medium bowl, whip the cream with the remaining 2 teaspoons sugar (more or less to taste) until it forms soft mounds.

To build the burgers, pipe thick, round cheesecake patties onto the bun bottoms. Top with the pineapple slices, pour over the raspberry purée, and top each with a generous dollop of whipped cream. Tuck a mint sprig in the cream and balance the bun tops against the side of the burgers. Serve immediately.

SHAKE & POUR

BURGER BAR MILKSHAKES

I've noticed that when it comes to burgers, even the most sophisticated palates revel in the combination of juicy burgers and indulgent milkshakes. We serve a lot of them and take the time to make them right: to order, with hand-scooped high-fat ice cream blended as they once were, with stick blenders. This amount is enough to make two smaller servings, but instead we serve the extra on the side in the frost-beaded metal blending container. They almost always come back to the kitchen empty. **Build your own:** Milkshakes offer a great opportunity for invention garnishing—colorful straws both plastic and edible, crushed nuts and colorful candies, chocolate curls, powdered cinnamon and cocoa; sprinkles and, of course, cherries—fresh, maraschino, or preserved sour cherries. For adult versions, add your favorite liquor and/or liquers.

MAKES 1 DRINK

$^1/_4$ cup heavy cream
1 teaspoon superfine sugar
Dash of vanilla extract
$1^1/_4$ cups premium ice cream (vanilla, strawberry, chocolate, etc.)

$^1/_3$ cup whole milk
1 teaspoon very finely chopped nuts
Chocolate curls

In a small bowl, whip the cream until frothy. Continue whipping, while adding the sugar gradually, until firm peaks form. Fold in the vanilla and set aside until needed. Pack the whipped cream into a pastry bag fitted with a star tip.

In a blender, blend the ice cream and milk until smooth. Pour into a tall glass, pipe on a generous mound of the whipped cream, add a straw, and garnish with the chopped nuts and chocolate curls. Serve any remaining shake on the side.

ROOT BEER FLOAT

When my wife and I were first in the United States, our English was still a bit shaky. We left our hotel one day to buy beer. Later, back in our room, we tasted it and were shocked. What was this American beer? We had bought root beer. Perhaps no American needs to be told how to make a root beer float, but they might need reminding that it's a beloved drink with burgers. To turn this simple confection into a real treat, seek out one of the artisanally produced root beers and use super-premium ice cream.

MAKES 1 DRINK

1 small bottle cold root beer	2 large scoops vanilla ice cream

Half fill a large, tall glass with root beer. Gently add the ice cream, and then top off with more root beer. Be careful that it does not foam over the edge of the glass. Serve with a fat straw and a long-handled spoon.

BROWN COW

Closely related to the root beer float, the brown cow is made with cola and a dash of chocolate syrup. There really is no polite way to enjoy a brown cow—whether you siphon up the sweet, milky cola and then spoon down the melty ice cream or slurp up a little ice cream with each spoonful of cola, it's all good.

MAKES 1 DRINK

2 tablespoons (1 ounce) chocolate sauce (page 00) or purchased chocolate syrup

1 small bottle cola
2 large scoops vanilla ice cream

In a large, tall glass, stir together the chocolate sauce and a splash of the cola. Half fill the glass with more cola and then gently add the ice cream. Serve with a fat straw and a long-handled spoon.

SIN CITY RED EYE

Our Burger Bar manager, Lisa Gourgeon, likes to create drinks with the many beers we have on tap. For this variation on the Bloody Mary, she uses a refreshing, crisp, lager-style beer from a local Las Vegas microbrewery, Sin City. Lisa advises using any beer you prefer. The cocktail makes a great companion to the Breakfast Burger (page 51).

MAKES 1 DRINK

Coarse salt

2 lime or lemon wedges

3 ounces Bloody Mary mix, V8 juice, or tomato juice

1½ ounces Skyy vodka

Splash of olive juice

Dash of freshly grated horseradish

Dash of freshly ground black pepper

Dash of Tabasco

Dash of Worcestershire sauce

Ice cubes

3 ounces Sin City Light beer

1 pimento-stuffed green olive

1 long wooden skewer

Pour some salt into a saucer. Wipe the rim of a chilled pint glass with a lime or lemon wedge and then upend the glass into the salt. Twist and turn the glass until the lip has a nice coating. Set the prepared glass aside. This can be done well in advance, a good idea when making drinks for a party.

Pour the Bloody Mary mix, vodka, olive juice, horseradish, pepper, Tabasco, and Worcestershire into an ice-filled cocktail shaker. Shake well and pour into the prepared glass. Float the beer on top. To garnish, thread the olive and the remaining lime wedge onto the skewer and set it in the drink.

CAIPIRINHA DE MARACUJA

The national drink of Brazil, the caipirinha ("little country girl" in Brazilian), combines the national spirit, cachaça—a clear spirit made from sugarcane—with plenty of lime. The drink now enjoys great popularity and, like the martini before it, has become the starting point for many variations. Passion fruit, *maracuja* in Brazilian, flavors this drink. You can always substitute white rum for cachaça. In Brazil, cachaça forms the base of many fruit drinks and is even used to flavor meat and fish stews.

MAKES 1 DRINK

1 whole lime, plus 1 lime wedge

4 teaspoons sugar

About 8 ice cubes

1½ ounces cachaça or white rum

½ ounce Grand Marnier

Pulp from ½ fresh passion fruit, or ½ ounce passion fruit purée

1 raspberry

1 long wooden skewer

1 lime or lemon twist

Quarter the lime lengthwise, and then cut it crosswise into ¼-inch-thick pieces. Put them in a cocktail shaker with the sugar. Using a muddler, crush them together well until the sugar dissolves. Add the ice cubes to the shaker and pour in the cachaça, Grand Marnier, and passion fruit. Close the shaker and shake lightly. Pour the contents into a tall, chilled glass. To garnish, thread the raspberry and lime wedge onto the skewer and set it in the drink. Balance the twist on the edge of the glass.

LAVENDER-CUCUMBER MOJITO

The mojito fuels many a Caribbean dance party. Born in Cuba, the drink has spread its influence throughout the Americas. Cucumber gives this summer version a thirst-quenching character, while the lavender adds a soothing, aromatic quality that stimulates the palate. If lavender is not available, you can try this with fresh mint or rosemary. Simple syrup is equal parts sugar and water boiled together for 5 minutes. Keep a supply in the fridge to speed your cocktail-making.

MAKES 1 DRINK

One 2-inch piece peeled cucumber
5 fresh mint leaves
Juice of 1 lime
$3/_4$ ounce simple syrup
About 6 ice cubes

2 ounces white rum
1 small pinch of dried lavender flowers
Club soda
1 sprig fresh lavender

Halve the cucumber lengthwise and scrape the seeds out with the tip of a spoon, then cut it into $1/_4$-inch chunks. Put them in a cocktail shaker with the mint, lime juice, and simple syrup. Using a muddler, mix the ingredients together just enough to break up the cucumber a bit. Add the ice cubes, rum, and lavender flowers; close the shaker tightly; and upend it once or twice just to mix lightly. Pour the contents into a tall, chilled glass, top off with a splash of club soda, and garnish with the lavender sprig.

MULATA

Our dining room manager and sommelier, Marcus Garcia, created this drink. Served in a martini glass with a sugar-and-salt-frosted rim, the cocktail seduces with its sweet, vanilla fragrance. Because the ingredients include white Brazilian rum (cachaça) and dark rum, he named the drink for the brown-skinned, large-eyed women of northern Brazil so famous for their beauty. This drink requires two homemade preparations: vanilla-infused salt and vanilla-infused cachaça. But these are easily made at home and can be used in a myriad of ways (see page 158). Look for agave nectar in natural food shops or Latin markets. See a photo of Marcus's creation on page 149.

MAKES 1 DRINK

1 teaspoon sugar
1 teaspoon Vanilla-Infused Sea Salt (page 158)
1 lime wedge
Juice of 1 lime
4 fresh mint leaves
1 teaspoon agave nectar or simple syrup
Ice cubes
4 ounces guava juice

1 ounce dark rum
1 ounce Vanilla-Infused Cachaça or white rum
   (page 158)
$^1/_2$ ounce passion fruit purée
$^1/_2$ ounce reposado tequila
Dash grenadine
1 orange slice
$^1/_2$ vanilla bean pod, split in half lengthwise

Pour the sugar and salt into a saucer and mix together lightly. Wipe the rim of a martini glass with the lime wedge and then upend the glass in the salt mixture. Twist and turn the glass until the lip has a nice coating. Set the prepared glass aside.

In a cocktail shaker, muddle together the lime juice, mint leaves, and agave nectar until the mint releases its fragrance. Fill the shaker with ice, add the guava juice, rum, cachaça, passion gruit puree, and tequila. Shake well and strain into the prepared glass. Carefully add a dash grenadine then thread the orange slice onto the vanilla bean and rest garnish on top of the glass.

VANILLA-INFUSED SALT & VANILLA-INFUSED CACHAÇA

Keep a bottle of the infused cachaça in the refrigerator or freezer. For a vanilla martini, simply pour the spirit into a chilled glass. Use it to give tropical drinks an unexpected, aromatic twist. You can infuse cachaça, white rum, or vodka, whatever is your preference. Vanilla is a surprisingly delicious addition to seafood dishes. You can use the salt or the alcohol to flavor lobster, jumbo shrimp, or scallops.

3 vanilla beans, split lengthwise
$^1/_4$ cup sea salt

One 750-ml bottle cachaça

To make the salt: Scrape the vanilla seeds from half of one of the vanilla beans and put them in a spice grinder or food processor with the salt. Reserve the pod. Blend until well mixed and pour into a glass jar. Store, tightly covered, at room temperature until needed.

To make the cachaça: Put the remaining $2^1/_2$ vanilla beans and the reserved half vanilla pod into the cachaça and leave at room temperature for 3 days. The spirit will become scented with vanilla and will take on a slight brown color from the beans. Refrigerate or freeze and use as needed. When the bottle is empty, simply refill with more cachaça and repeat the maceration. You can refill the bottle twice before needing to replace the vanilla beans.

GOLDEN CHAMPAGNE COCKTAIL

This very pretty, elegant cocktail turns any occasion into a special event. The rising bubbles dance with edible gold flakes. You can find gold flakes in specialty food stores, sometimes in a shaker and sometimes as thin foil on small, paper squares. Use the very best spirits—aged Grand Marnier and cognac and a sparkling wine with rich, complex flavors.

MAKES 1 DRINK

1 sugar cube
3 drops Angostura bitters
$^1/_2$ ounce aged cognac
$^1/_4$ ounce Grand Marnier Cuvée du Centenaire

About 4 ounces brut Champagne or sparkling wine
1 raspberry
23-carat gold flakes

Soak the sugar cube with the bitters and drop it into a chilled flute glass. Add the cognac and Grand Marnier and then fill the glass with Champagne. Drop in the raspberry and dust the top of the drink with a few shakes of the gold flakes, or, if you find large pieces, simply float a single large flake on top.

CHOCOLATE MARTINI

After a burger feast, you might want something light, yet spirited. This cocktail does double duty as an after-dinner drink and as a dessert. If you would like to make your own truffles, try the recipe for the Chocolate Hazelnut Burger (page 140).

MAKES 1 DRINK

2 ounces vanilla-infused vodka (page 158)
Splash of dark crème de cacao
Splash of Kahlúa

Ice cubes
1 chocolate truffle

Pour the vodka, crème de cacao, and Kahlúa into an ice-filled cocktail shaker. Shake well and strain into a chilled martini glass. Drop in the chocolate truffle.

APPLE PIE MARTINI

This version appeals for its fresh, bright taste and makes a great drink for summer parties. The brand of vodka that we use, Cîroc, is unusual because it is made from grapes. It is especially good in cocktails because its smooth flavor doesn't compete with other ingredients. You can make the drink with any premium vodka. The green apple and pineapple purées add sweet-tart flavors.

MAKES 1 DRINK

Cinnamon sugar
1 lemon wedge
1 1/2 ounces Cîroc vodka
1/2 ounce green apple purée
Dash of pineapple purée

Squeeze of fresh lemon juice
Ice cubes
2 unpeeled green apple slices, cut as thinly as possible on a mandoline

Pour some cinnamon sugar into a saucer. Wipe the rim of a chilled martini glass with the lemon wedge and then upend the glass into the sugar. Twist and turn the glass until the lip has a nice coating. Set the prepared glass aside.

Pour the vodka, apple and pineapple purées, and lemon juice into an ice-filled cocktail shaker. Shake well and strain into the prepared glass. Float the apple slices on top of the drink.

There are at least two ways to approach matching burgers and beer. The first is to eat what you like and drink what you like. You will be sure to enjoy yourself. But if you suspect that even more pleasure and fun might be had with slightly more thoughtful selections, then let a few general principles guide you.

Balance: Burgers and beer make a natural, and winning, combination. They share a sense of fun as well as a democratic spirit—approachable and accessible. But taste argues even more powerfully for the match. Beer's blend of sweet, bitter, and bubbly can freshen and clear the palate between big bites of rich, sweet meat, tangy condiments, and salty fries. The interplay of the basic components that give beer its style and flavor—malt, hops, yeast, fermentation temperature, carbonation—balances the flavors of burgers.

Light with white; dark with red: Ales and lagers follow separate paths on their way to becoming beer. Those differences allow them to play distinct roles in food pairing. Lagers, cold fermented and then kept cold during their conditioning before bottling, generally grow up to be crisp and bright. They pair with lighter foods such as fish, white meats like chicken, and salads. Ales, on the other hand, are fermented warm and are usually aged only briefly. They tend to display bigger flavors that can be fruity, earthy, and strong. Match these with richer, heavier dishes such as beef and lamb burgers. There is enough validity to this general rule to make it a great place to begin tasting.

Aromatic harmonies: Burgers can contain a world of flavors. Beer can too. The varieties of hops and malts and how they are handled add amazing complexity to beer flavors. Beer can display caramelized and roasted flavors, even chocolate and coffee notes from the malts used. They can have floral, fruity, herbal, and citrus notes derived from hops and fermentation yeasts. Some beers are even brewed with spices and citrus zest. Matching the aromatic qualities of burgers and beers can lead to new and exciting pairings.

Style: There is, of course, no better way to know how a beer tastes than to drink it. But the label provides many clues to a beer's style and thus its flavor profile. It tells you whether the beer is an ale, a lager, or something else, perhaps a lambic or a seasonal brew. The label might also describe the flavors and how the beer is made.

Refreshment: Bubbles and bitterness give beer its amazing ability to refresh your palate. The carbonation and characteristic bitterness of hops cut through foods that otherwise coat your tongue, such as eggs, cheese, and fat from meat. They can restore your ability to taste and thus extract maximum pleasure from every bite.

Compare and contrast: Thank goodness, no thesis on the subject of beer and burgers is required. But the concept of complementary and contrasting flavors does apply. For example, you can match the Black Jack Burger (page 13)—sweet meat, caramelized flavors from grilling or sautéing, earthy and pungent flavors of tapenade, rich flavors of melting cheese—with a rich Belgian double ale. Its dark, complex flavors balance the tapenade; its sweet flavors play off the sweet meat; and the bubbles and fairly high alcohol, 8 percent, cut through rich meat and cheese.

I before E, except after C: In an exception (and there are lots of delicious exceptions) to the light/lager with white, etc., rule, amber lagers also make good companions to red-meat burgers. They are medium bodied with some sweetness from caramelized malts and have plenty of brisk hop flavor and carbonation to keep the palate refreshed.

Matching intensities: Take as an example the Chocolate-Hazelnut Burger (page 140). Impossible to match, you say? Very dark malts can have bracing, deep flavors that allow the beer to act the role of an espresso. An imperial stout, for instance, can have chocolate and coffee flavors, making it a great choice to pair with the dessert burger. The pairing would exemplify not only aroma and flavor affinities, but also a balance of intensities of flavor, both in the beer and in the dessert.

Balance the dominant ingredient: But which one is it? In the Pesto Beef Burger (page 20), is it the beef or the pesto? In the Brazilian Rock Shrimp Burger (page 77), is the primary ingredient the rock shrimp or the flavorings—coconut milk, cilantro, ginger, garlic? In both these cases, the way to begin hunting for truly great pairings would be to focus on the strongest flavors—the pesto, for instance, and the shrimp burger's flavorings.

Learn from the locals: Every cuisine and culture has its beer. So if your burger has Mexican flavors, for instance, you might choose a Mexican beer. Have fun seeking out some new ones to try.

INDEX

Martinis
   Apple Pie Martini, 161
   Chocolate Martini, 160
Mayonnaise, green peppercorn and
   lemon, 126
Milkshakes, burger bar, *150*, 151
Mojito, lavender-cucumber, 156
Mulata, 157
Mushroom Beef Burger, 23–24
Mustard, old-fashioned, 129
Mustard Seed Chicken Burger, *54*,
   55–56

N

New York Strip Surprise Burger, The,
   34–35

O

Old-Fashioned Mustard, 129
Onion(s)
   grilled, steaks, 105
   pickled, grenadine, 134
   rings, beer-battered, Alsace, 106,
     107
Open-Faced Chicken Burger, 57–59
Ostrich Bacon Burger, 63–65
Oven Fries, *100*, 101

P

Panisse Fries, 102–103, *103*
Perfect French Fries, *96*, 97
Pesto, cilantro-arugula, 127
Pesto Beef Burger, 20–22
Pickled onions, grenadine, 134
Pickled vegetables, Brazilian, *110*,
   111–112

Pickles, beet, 113
Pillard, Laurent, ix, x, 146
Piquillo Pepper Ketchup, 132
Pork burgers. *See also* BLT Turkey
   Club Burger
   Breakfast Burger, 51–52, *52*
   Feijoada Burger, 43–45
Provençal Burger, 46–47

Q

Quick Chicken Stock, 7
Quinoa, roasted squash-, burger,
   87–88

R

Red Wine, Thyme, and Shallot
   Sauce, 136
Relish, red pepper–tomato, spicy,
   130–131
Roasted Squash-Quinoa Burger,
   87–88
Root Beer Float, 152
Rouas, Maurice, ix

S

Salads
   Creamy Cucumber Salad, 115
   Endive-Apple Salad, 122
   Heirloom Cherry Tomato Salad, 117
   Marinated Fennel Salad, 114
   Marinated Vegetable Salad, 116
Salmon burgers
   Double Salmon Tartare Burger,
     71–72
   Salmon Fillet Burger, 73–75
Salsa, grilled avocado-mango, *118*, 119

Sauces, 123–137. *See also* Chocolate
   Sauce; Grilled Avocado-Mango
   Salsa; Sesame Vinaigrette;
   Tartare Dressing
   Caramelized Shallot Jam, 133
   Cilantro-Arugula Pesto, 127
   Fried Herbs, 137
   Green Peppercorn and Lemon May-
     onnaise, 126
   Grenadine Pickled Onions, 134
   Old-Fashioned Mustard, 129
   Piquillo Pepper Ketchup, 132
   Red Wine, Thyme, and Shallot
     Sauce, 136
   Shallot-Tarragon Butter, 135
   Spicy Aïoli, 125
   Spicy Red Pepper–Tomato Relish,
     130–131
   Tapenade, 128
Seafood burgers, 67–81
   Brazilian Rock Shrimp Burger, *76*,
     77–78
   Crab Sliders, 79–81
   Double Salmon Tartare Burger,
     71–72
   Salmon Fillet Burger, 73–75
   Seared Tuna Burger, 69–70
Seared Tuna Burger, 69–70
Sea salt, about, 8
Sesame Vinaigrette, 69
Shallot-Tarragon Butter, 135
Short rib–stuffed burgers. *See* New
   York Strip Surprise Burger
Shrimp, rock, burger, Brazilian, *76*,
   77–78
Side dishes, 95–122. *See also* Salads
   Alsace Beer-Battered Onion Rings,
     106, *107*
   Beet Pickles, 113
   Brazilian Pickled Vegetables, *110*,
     111–112
   Fruit Fries, 120, *121*

BLACK JACK BURGER BLUE CHEESE-STUFF BACON SLIDERS BUR AND FRIES PESTO BE BURGER MUSHROOM BEEF BURGER SURF URF BURGER BURG AU POIVRE BLACK AN BLUE BURGER THEN YORK STRIP SURPRIS BURGER FLEUR BURG WITH TRUFFLES BUF ALO BURGER FEIJOA BURGER PROVENCAL